25 TOP BLUES ROCK SONGS

T0065957

TAB+ = TAB + TONE + TECHNIQUE

This is not your typical guitar tab book. In the new *Tab+* series from Hal Leonard, we provide you guidance on how to capture the guitar tones for each song as well as tips and advice on the techniques used to play the songs.

Where possible, we've confirmed the gear used on the original recordings via new and previously published interviews with the guitarists, producers, and/or engineers. Then we make general recommendations on how to achieve a similar tone, based on that info. You'll note that we do not mention specific modeling or software amps, as those units will typically contain models for the original amps we do cite.

Some of the songs herein will be easy to play even for advanced beginner players, whereas others present a much greater challenge. In either case, we've identified key techniques in each song that should help you learn the song with greater ease.

ISBN 978-1-4803-5571-2

HAL•LEONARD®
CORPORATION
7777 W. BLUEMOUND RD. P.O. BOX 13819 MILWAUKEE, WI 53213

Visit Hal Leonard Online at
www.halleonard.com

PERFORMANCE NOTES TAB. TONE. TECHNIQUE.

By Dave Rubin

BE CAREFUL WITH A FOOL

Johnny Winter

This epic slow blues was featured on Winter's self-titled, "official" debut (#200, 1969), following his discovery in Texas in 1968. The cathartic slow drag cover of a B.B. King classic shows both his debt to the master and his overwhelming, heretofore unheard "white hot" technique. Blues and blues-rock guitarists took note, either running for cover or to the woodshed to practice.

TONE

Before acquiring his iconic non-reverse Firebirds, Winter experimented with various axes including a late sixties Fender Electric XII 12-string solid body electric converted to a 6-string. A tweed 4x10 Fender Bassman, long the revered "chesty" blues amp of the *cognoscenti*, complemented the single-coil pickups. A Strat or Tele set on the bridge pickup, straight into a 20 to 50-watt tube combo amp with volume at 7, treble at 10, middle at 5 and bass at 4 should create the required edge.

TECHNIQUE

Winter does not just play blindingly fast, he plays with a particular rhythmic picking technique resulting in a swing feel not possessed by some of his peers or contemporary blues guitar heroes. Part of it may be attributed to his use of a plastic thumbpick, which he utilizes to efficiently execute the critical alternating down and up pick strokes. He also uses fewer hammer-ons and pull-offs than other speedsters. Measure 1 of the Intro contains a fine example of this sound as he varies his attack for a dynamic effect and may be heard even in the blistering measure 3 of stop-time. However, he makes an exception in measures 1and 2 in the second and third Verses, where he employs all down strokes for the eighth notes to produce a punchy, driving sound.

BORN IN CHICAGO

Paul Butterfield Band

Despite Alan Lomax introducing them as a "bunch of white boys who think they can play the blues" when the Paul Butterfield Blues Band backed the infamous electric Bob Dylan at the 1965 Newport Jazz Festival, they were bi-racial and revolutionary, featuring guitarists Mike Bloomfield and Elvin Bishop. "Born in Chicago" appropriately led off their self-titled debut (#123, 1965).

TONE

Bloomfield, arguably the first guitar hero, used a 1964 rosewood fingerboard Telecaster through a prototype Guild Thunderbird amp, which was known for emitting a special distortion when it overheated, while Bishop played his iconic "Red Dog," a 1962 Gibson ES-345 through a pre-CBS, blackface Fender amp. "Bloomers" is picking his single-coil bridge pickup while Bishop is likely strumming on both humbuckers with the Varitone set on position 1. A 12 to15-watt tube amp with a 10" or 12" speaker cranked, and a 50-watt or larger 2x12 combo with the controls at "5" or so, should get their sound, respectively.

TECHNIQUE

Bloomfield (Gtr. 1) plays the single-note riff and solos while Bishop (Gtr. 2) comps the fat, dominant 6-string barre chords. The former would evolve his style to where he improvised creatively in the composite blues scale and the minor modes. However, in the Guitar Solo and Outro-Guitar Solo he stayed true to the A minor pentatonic scale in a few positions. Taking his cue from B.B. King, he was an expressive string bender with snaky vibrato. Use the ring finger backed up by the middle and index for virtually all the bends in the solos, maintaining steady pressure during the vibrato to extract maximum sustain.

BRIDGE OF SIGHS
Robin Trower

The British blues-rock virtuoso's second solo outing, the gold *Bridge of Sighs* (#10, 1974), was a smash as Trower won Guitarist of the Year honors from *Guitar Player* magazine. A masterpiece of post-Hendrix chord melody and soloing, it sent a loud, sensuous, distorted signal to guitarists to once again improvise extensively and without inhibition in the age of the sensitive singer/songwriters beloved by cranky, tin-eared critics.

TONE
The unearthly molten lava tone originated from a choice of vintage Strats (in the out-of-phase notch between the neck and middle pickups) connected to a 100-watt Marshall stack via a Univox Univibe and a Dan Armstrong Red Ranger treble booster. However, even a small, 20-watt tube combo with reverb and the bass "dimed," with a quality distortion box, can achieve similar results when coupled with the critical component, the Univibe or like copy available today.

TECHNIQUE
For the signature riff in measures 1–4 of the Intro, trill the E note on the 4th string with the strong middle finger, slide from A♯ to B with the index, barre the D/G double stop on strings 2 and 1 with the ring finger and execute the double-stop, half-step bend of A/C♯ on strings 3 and 2 with the index finger. In order to perform a reasonable facsimile of measures 7 through 10 of the second Interlude with one guitar, just play the downstemmed part notated on the 5th and 4th strings.

BROKE DOWN ON THE BRAZOS
Gov't Mule

Appearing as the opening track on the eighth studio album (#34, 2009) by the blues-rock and jam band powerhouse, it was actually the last one written. It features ZZ Top guitar slinger Billy Gibbons in the outro dual with Warren Haynes. It also represents the recorded debut of new bassist Jorgen Carlsson. Haynes, along with Derek Trucks, had recently announced his resignation from the Allman Brothers Band in order to pursue his various musical interests.

TONE
In a Les Paul lover's fantasy come to life, Haynes handles his signature LP and Gibbons also slings one of Uncle Lester's creations. The "Muleskinner" overheats the tubes on a Fender Pro Junior while Billy punishes an unidentified Marshall clone. To get their Texas raunch, a Les Paul Standard is highly recommended. However, a humbucking PRS or similar heavyweight solid body 6-string on the bridge pickup could suffice when mated with a compact tube combo like the Pro Junior floored, with the guitar volume adjusted to taste.

TECHNIQUE
Note that all guitars are in drop D tuning and down one whole step with Gtr. 1 (Haynes rhythm) producing a roaring, nasty bass string sound. The first Interlude should be approached as classic sixteenth-note funk with steady, down and up pick strokes and mutes where indicated. The extended Outro-Solo, however, is where all the good stuff happens as Gibbons and Haynes (Gtrs. 4 and 2, respectively) have way too much fun trading blues barbs. With the D minor pentatonic scale (sounding as C minor pentatonic) as typically fertile improvisational territory, they produce a veritable blues guitar workshop in their skillful navigation of all positions.

COME ON, PT. 1
Jimi Hendrix

Arguably the greatest rock guitarist of all time, Jimi Hendrix needs no introduction. His third and final album with the original Experience, *Electric Ladyland* (#1, 1968), has come to be regarded as his masterpiece. The raw, funky, hard rocking cover of the Earl King R&B classic was a last minute and welcome addition to complete the double album.

TONE
A late-sixties CBS Strat on the bridge pickup, through perhaps a Fender Dual Showman with a Dallas-Arbiter Fuzz Face at a moderate setting (and a Vox wah pedal in the solo), are the key ingredients for what sounds to be a "live" in the studio performance. To duplicate the sound, a Strat and a Fuzz Face seem obligatory, with perhaps a 20-watt Deluxe Reverb with the 'verb shut down, the treble at 8 and the bass at 4.

TECHNIQUE
Try accessing the clanging double-stop in the Intro by barring the G and B notes with the index finger for the Em chord, and the middle and index (low to high) for the F♯/A over the D chord. The coolest element on a cool track, however, is

the tri-tone inversion that occurs in measures 1 and 2 of the Chorus while shifting from the E7#9 chord to A13. It's one of the hippest I-IV moves known to guitarists. Simply finger it index, middle, and ring (low to high) and be aware that it is moveable to other keys. The Outro-Guitar Solo is a tutorial in maximizing blues-approved expression in the root octave position of the E minor pentatonic scale. Crucial to the execution is the index finger barring various combinations of strings at the 12th fret, allowing the ring and pinky fingers do their work. Dig his quote from Freddie King's "San-Ho-Zay" in measures 1 through 8.

CROSSFIRE
Stevie Ray Vaughan

In Step (#33, 1989) was Stevie Ray's last studio album with Double Trouble and contains the #1 Mainstream Rock Tracks hit, "Crossfire." It won the Grammy for Best Contemporary Blues Album that year. His influence on blues and rock guitarists has been immense, and his tragic death in a helicopter accident in 1990 was an inestimable loss for the blues and rock communities. His big Texas boots are yet to be filled.

TONE

Vaughan could be obsessive about his tone as evidenced by the 32 amps he had at his disposal for the album sessions. A video shows him playing his beloved "#1" Strat set in the notch between the neck and middle pickups through what might be a pair of black face Fender Super Reverbs. That said, if you want something approaching the real deal, string your Strat with .013–.052 gauges, tune down a half step, adjust an Ibanez TS-9 Tube Screamer for high level and low drive, and play through a 20 to 40-watt tube combo with the volume at 10, treble at 8, bass at 4 and the guitar volume at whatever level your neighbors will tolerate.

TECHNIQUE

In Step represented his further evolution away from straight 12-bar blues with "Crossfire" being a stirring example of the deep grooves he was after. Be sure to see the fingering direction on the transcription below measures 1 and 2 in the Intro for Riff A. In addition, for the numerous double-string bends on strings 3 and 2 throughout, pull down with the ring finger. Lastly, for the searing, repeating bend and vibrato of A to B on the 1st string, 17th fret in the first measure of the Outro-Guitar Solo, be aware that Vaughan used his ring finger backed up his middle and index, removing his thumb from the back of the neck and shaking the string by moving his arm up and down from the elbow for a most vigorous effect.

GOING DOWN
Jeff Beck Group

The 2.0 and last version of the JBG on the "orange" album (#9, 1972) benefitted from the production of soul man Steve Cropper in Memphis and featured a hard-driving version of the Don Nix blues rock classic. After *Beck, Bogert & Appice* in 1973, it would be the last time the great "El Becko" led a group with a lead singer until he reunited with Rod Stewart in 1985 while convening a spectacular solo career playing instrumentals.

TONE

Besides being a virtuoso and an incomparably inventive rock guitar god, Beck is a tone guru. The album likely debuts his earliest defection from his iconic Les Paul Standard to a Strat. A video with the group from 1972 shows him playing the tune on a maple board, whammy bar, pre-CBS model on the bridge pickup through a Marshall stack. A Strat hooked to a smaller, master volume equipped Marshall tube amp (or even a medium-sized Fender or Mesa Boogie with master volume) and a stomp box like a Tube Screamer with the drive boosted will get you "going down."

TECHNIQUE

Beck is a master of phrasing and dynamics. Take note of his dramatic musical rests throughout. Along with his tasty, authentic blues licks gleaned from the G minor pentatonic scale, there are any number of Beck-isms to learn. In measures 7 and 8 of the Intro he emits "cries" through his guitar by quickly jabbing F (♭7th) one step up to G (root) with his ring finger, backed by his middle and index fingers, and releasing back to F. Following is the F to G bend across the bar line and a dynamic, zippy series of pull-offs and hammer-ons on the 1st string with the ring (B♭) and index (G) fingers. Showing hints of whammy bar magic to come is the dramatic, stunning dive bomb down to E in measures 10 and 11. Observe how Beck ends the phrase on an F, not allowing the bar to completely return to G. Measure 1 of the Guitar Solo contains one of his signature moves as he trills like a jackhammer from G to B♭ on the 3rd string with the middle finger while slowly dipping the bar down to D and back.

GOING UP THE COUNTRY

Canned Heat

The counterculture blues band of scholars – their name drawn from the Tommy Johnson 1928 classic "Canned Heat" – scored a hippie anthem (#11, 1968) when it was released as a single from their album, *Living the Blues*. Based significantly on "Bull Doze Blues" by Henry Thomas from 1928, it would be their highest-charting release as they perpetuated the endless boogie to the delight of the Woodstock generation.

TONE

Videos from the era show rhythm guitarist and band leader Alan Wilson fingerpicking a circa 1954 Les Paul Goldtop with P-90 pickups and combination/bar tailpiece, as well as a Telecaster. It has been reported that lead guitarist Henry Vestine played a "lightly amplified" electric on the studio recording. However, these gear concerns are academic. Virtually any solid body electric on the neck pickup at very low volume with no distortion through a 20 to 40-watt amp or larger, also at low volume with no distortion, will produce the desired folk/blues results.

TECHNIQUE

If playing in the original key of B♭ as per Gtr. 1, capo at the 8th fret as indicated and strum with bare fingers. Alternately, strum down (with the thumb) and up (with the index) on open position chord voicings. Observe how the melodic Intro and two Flute Solos have the "pan pipes" transcribed for guitar in the B♭ composite blues scale (blues scale + Mixolydian mode).

GREEN LIGHT GIRL

Doyle Bramhall II & Smokestack

Described as Eric Clapton's "secret weapon" and a member of the Arc Angels, Doyle Bramhall II is a relatively unsung blues-rock guitar hero with unimpeachable credentials. His heart-pounding eighth-note houserocker (#33, Mainstream Rock Tracks) was featured on *Welcome* (#45 Heatseekers, 2001), his third solo album, rereleased in 2008.

TONE

Bramhall punishes a rosewood board Strat into Marshall 100-watt Super Bass heads with 2x12 cabs in a manner similar and familiar to all great contemporary Texas guitar slingers, though he also employs an expansive pedal board subject to frequent change. The Crest Audio Fuzz Face or the Analog Man NKT Sun Face may have been his main distortion box at this time. A Strat on the bridge pickup though a high gain amp (Marshall, Mesa Boogie or any number of muscular boutique amps), boosted by a modern tube-type stomp box, adjusted appropriately, will create the classic raw roar.

TECHNIQUE

Bramhall is left-handed and plays a left-handed Strat strung righty, resulting in his pulling *down* on his treble strings alá Albert King and Otis Rush, to produce vigorous bends and whiplash vibrato. The drop D tuning for Gtr. 2 makes playing the open string D5 power chords on strings 6 and 5 a cinch. Check out the way Bramhall indicates a modulation from Dm7 in the verses to D5 in the Guitar Solo by inserting a D major first inversion triad into measures 1 and 2 followed by an implied D7 triple-stop in measure 4 for the all-important blues vibe.

THE GREEN MANALISHI

Fleetwood Mac

B.B. King famously called Peter Green the "only guitarist to ever make me sweat" and the innumerable other players who have come under his black magic spell can well understand. The last song he wrote, while a member of Fleetwood Mac, made an impressive showing (#10, 1970). He has claimed the nightmarish composition, revealed to him in an LSD-induced dream, is about the evils of money.

TONE

Though he played a maple neck 1959 Strat on occasion, Green is known for his iconic 1959 Les Paul 'Burst. Due to the magnet being reversed in one pickup, it produced a funky, out-of-phase tone with the selector switch in the middle position. Like Clapton, who preceded him in the Bluesbreakers, he favored the Marshall JTM 45 combo at first, followed by an Orange/Matamp, a Fender Twin, and eventually a Dual Showman as on the studio recording. While most guitarists will not alter the pickup on their LP, it is the signature tone when both pickups are in play. Up to the Interlude, fire up a black face (or silver face) Twin Reverb or Super Reverb, put the treble on 6, the middle on 5, the bass on 5 and the reverb on 4. Crank it, or, in lieu of the likely oppressive volume, utilize a stomp box to dial in the proper amount of edgy distortion without overdoing and compressing the sound. For the Interlude and Gtr. 3 (Danny Kirwan also on a vintage 'Burst and seen with an Orange stack in videos), peg the reverb and switch to the bridge pickup.

TECHNIQUE
For Gtr. 1 (Danny Kirwan) in the Intro, use your index and ring fingers for the power chords in measures 1 and 2 and then slide your index down to the 5th fret on the 5th string in measures 3 and 4, being careful to not mute the open 6th string. In measures 5 and 6, barre your index finger at the 2nd fret while using your ring finger on the 4th fret of the 5th string, again being careful to not mute the open 6th string. Observe how in measures 9–12 of the Interlude one guitar could play both Rhy. Fig. 2 and the Gtr. 4 part: Strum the Em voicing for the duration of an eighth note on beats 1 and 3 of each measure, followed by the licks starting on the second eighth note of beats 1 and 3 in each measure. In measures 13 and 14, just include the E octave on strings 5 and 6. As for Gtr. 4, (starting in measure 15 of the Outro) it is not necessary to duplicate Green's licks verbatim. Just internalize their feel and spirit while expressing oneself in the E Aeolian mode.

THE HUNTER
Free

Free, the British blues rockers featuring vocalist Paul Rodgers and unsung blues guitar hero Paul Kossoff (both age 18), formed in 1968. Their debut album, *Tons of Sobs* (1969), contained the Booker T. & The M.G.'s song recently recorded by Albert King on his monumental *Born Under a Bad Sign* album. When the band broke up in 1973, Rodgers and drummer Simon Kirke went on to form Bad Company with Mott the Hoople guitarist Mick Ralphs and King Crimson bassist Boz Burrell. Kossoff led Back Street Crawler before tragically dying from his heroin addiction in 1976.

TONE
Kossoff was another in the line of great British blues guitarists wielding a 1959 sunburst Les Paul, seen with the pickguard removed, through a Marshall Super Lead/Bass or PA stack, or an Orange amp, though he may have played an obscure Selmer T&B 50 in the studio (as is rumored for "All Right Now"). A good quality humbucker-powered solid body guitar played on the bridge pickup through a Marshall or other high gain tube amp would be the perfect combination to begin to build his tone.

TECHNIQUE
Kossoff was a relative minimalist who was all about bending and vibrato; his speed and expressiveness with the latter technique at such a tender age is remarkable. He rarely, if ever, used his pinky, instead bending with his ring or middle finger. In measures 1 and 3 of the Intro, he bends the D to E with his ring finger backed up by the middle and index, landing on the A note (3rd string, 2nd fret) with his strong middle finger where he blisters the fret with his whip-like vibrato. In measures 15 through 19 of the Guitar Solo, he bends D to E on the 2nd string with his middle finger, accessing G on the 1st string with his ring finger, and really laying into the bent E with wicked vibrato in one of his signature moves. In measure 39, play the F#/C double stop with the middle and ring fingers respectively to efficiently set up the hand for the Kossoff style: Hit the A note on the 1st string with the index and bend the G on the 2nd string with the ring finger. As they say, "It's all in the wrist."

JUST GOT PAID
ZZ Top

Their second album, *Rio Grande Mud* (#104, 1972), was considered a commercial disappointment. Nonetheless, it heralded the arrival of arguably the most devastatingly powerful blues-rock trio ever, led by the sensational guitarist Billy "Rev. Willie G" Gibbons. The Stones-y single "Francine" (#69) was a respectable hit, but "Just Got Paid" blew the barn doors open for players and fans everywhere with its hard-edged, funky rhythms and smoking slide solo.

TONE
Not to be overlooked, Gibbons used to pick with a Mexican peso on super light .008–.040 strings at the recommendation of B.B. King. Mistress Pearly Gates, his iconic '59 'Burst sounds like the source of the righteous tone. Gibbons was known to be fond of using an 18-watt Marshall with a 2x12 cab containing 20-watt Celestion greenback speakers, though as late as 2008 he was still swearing by his 1968 100-watt Marshall plexi Super Lead. Then again, he recorded "La Grange" a year later on a tweed Fender Champ, so a brown tolex Fender Deluxe is the best guess for this tune. Hence a small, non-master volume tube combo set to 7 or 8 on the volume, 7 for treble, and 8 for bass, connected straight to a humbucking solid body – preferably an LP on the bridge pickup – should get it for the rhythm. For the slide fills and solo, run the volume flat out and boost the treble to 10. Vintage videos show Gibbons with a metal slide on his middle finger in order to access the rhythm licks. He now has a line of signature Pyrex glass slides.

TECHNIQUE

The secret to this "Top" classic is the open E tuning, making for compact accompaniment as provided by Gtr. 1, and seen in Riffs A and B, where only the index and ring fingers are necessary at frets 3 and 5, respectively. In addition, check out Gtr. 2 throughout to see how major chord forms are easily played in open E tuning with the index finger at the same fret positions as in standard tuning (as opposed to open G or D tuning). Similarly, the accompaniment of Gtr. 1 in the Guitar Solo is located around the 12th fret, with B/D double stop (♭7th/5th) at the 15th fret (accessed with the pinky in a small barre) implying E7. The Guitar Solo is essentially a "modal solo" based around the E (I) chord where Gibbons (Gtr. 2) phrases with true blues authenticity. However, do not miss how he regularly acknowledges the A (IV) chord with the root note at the 10th fret on the 2nd string even as he creates wave after wave of musical tension followed by release to the root note of E.

LEFT OVERS
Joe Bonamassa

Joe Bonamassa is unapologetic for being influenced more significantly by sixties British blues guitarists than their American forebears. Since 2000, the former child prodigy has blazed his own path to the top; the accomplishments of his ongoing career stand as evidence. Selected from the originals and classic covers album *Blues Deluxe* (#8 Top Blues Albums, 2003) – the title itself an homage to a Jeff Beck song from 1967 – this Albert Collins instrumental shuffle gets the hell rocked out of it.

TONE

Bonamassa was mentored by Tele virtuoso Danny Gatton and has been known to play one on occasion – as would be appropriate on this "Master of the Telecaster" tune – however, he may have been playing an ES-335 on the bridge pickup. He is also a true gear head who could rival Billy Gibbons, and he delivers the goods to prove it. Famous for a Marshall stack/vintage Fender combination live, in the studio it was reported he used a Budda Superdrive 30 and a Marshall Silver Jubilee 2555 when playing a Gibson. Conversely, it could be a Fender Princeton amplifying his '65 Strat on the bridge pickup in conjunction with a Carl Martin Hot Drive and Boost. This guitar/amp/stomp box combo could definitely reproduce the "cool sound" of a Telecaster. Also, take into account Bonamassa plays .011–.052 gauge strings for a naturally fat tone, and to reduce his tendency to shred.

TECHNIQUE

Albert Collins employed a capo and tuned to open Fm as a prime element of his signature sound, but Bonamassa does a fine approximation in standard tuning sans the clamp. Know that the "feel" and timing are most important in the unaccompanied eight-measure Intro derived from the C composite blues scale (blues scale + Mixolydian mode). Tapping one's foot is highly suggested in order to set and keep the tempo true. For the classic Collins-ism found in the Guitar Solo in measures 9 through 11 of the second 12-bar chorus, try vibratoing the root (C) with your index finger while keeping your other fingers *and thumb* off and away from the neck, waving in the air alá B.B. King. In the fourth chorus of the solo, execute the repeating two-beat pattern by barring strings 4, 3 and 2 at the 8th fret with your index finger, utilizing it not only for the E♭/G dyad, but for the B♭ note on the 4th string as well. Then use your ring finger to fret the adjacent C notes while you reiterate the riff against the changes of the 12-bar progression.

LIE TO ME
Jonny Lang

A true *wunderkind* from Fargo, ND, Jonny Lang began playing guitar at 12 and by the age of 16 released his major label debut, *Lie to Me* (#1 Blues and #44 Billboard Top 200, 1997). The single (#12 Mainstream Rock) and album revealed a young man blessed with a voice like Wilson Pickett and authentic blues guitar chops beyond his years. His conversion to Christianity in 2000 resulted in a series of religious albums, though on *Fight for My Soul* in 2013 he turned to R&B, soul and funk while maintaining a sense of spirituality.

TONE

Lang originally played a Benedict Tele-type guitar with two humbuckers and a P-90 in between. Subsequently he became identified with a 1972 Fender Thinline Tele after *Lie to Me* and later his signature Gibson Les Paul model. Two reissue Fender Deluxe Reverb amps, a Dallas-Arbiter Fuzz Face and a reissue Vox wah pedal comprised his basic road gear. A Tele or Strat on the bridge pickup through a 20 to 40-watt Fender combo with a high-gain stomper like the Fuzz Face or similar boost will provide the required fire power.

TECHNIQUE

Check out the Intro vamp played by Gtr. 1. It's the hammer-on–pull-off combinations that lead to the B5 chords, and the hammer-ons into the E5 chords that give the riff distinction. Pay close attention to the rhythmic timing. The silence between the chords, is essential to this funky groove. Lang (Gtr. 2) plays with a pick and bare fingers, not hybrid style, but in a 50/50 split. When utilizing his fingers, he uses both the thumb and middle finger while hiding the pick in the crook of his index finger. Sometimes he rests his thumb on the 6th string while up-picking with his middle finger. Even when using a pick, he has a propensity for up stokes. Lang is also rightly acknowledged for his fast, wide, expressive vibrato, produced by shaking the guitar up and down similar to Stevie Ray Vaughan.

LIVING IN A DREAM
Arc Angels

Formed in the early nineties in Austin, Texas (following the tragic death of Stevie Ray Vaughan), guitarist/singers Doyle Bramhall II and Charlie Sexton formed Arc Angels – taking their name from the initials of the Austin Rehearsal Complex – and recruited the Double Trouble rhythm section in a project holding out great promise. Their self-titled album (#127, 1992) was released to critical acclaim, but unfortunately the group imploded in 1994 due to Bramhall's heroin habit and inter-band conflict. In 2009 they reunited, minus bassist Tommy Shannon, touring and planning a second album – as yet unrecorded. They toured North America, Europe and Australia in 2013-14.

TONE

Both Bramhall and Sexton are confirmed gear nuts extending to guitars, amps and effects, and they likely used an array of it on their debut album. Judging by videos from the era, a reasonable assumption could be Bramhall, a lefty, playing one of his Strats – perhaps the red Charley Wirz custom copy with the lefty body and the righty neck – through a '68 Marshall Super Bass. Sexton plays a Rickenbacker 12-string electric (likely the 1993 model) through a Vox AC-50 bass amp. To reproduce their heavenly sound, the 12-string Ric is a necessity. For Sexton's fat, ringing rhythm parts, plug into a 40 to 50-watt tube combo, preferably of British nationality. A Strat on the bridge pickup through a Marshall stack or combo (even a little 15-watt Haze) will get Bramhall's rhythm and lead mojo.

TECHNIQUE

See how Sexton (Gtr. 2) tends to play minimal, open position chord forms on the middle strings. This approach limits some of the high frequencies, which could infringe on the sonic space of the vocals, plus the low frequencies of the middle strings are well above the bass's domain. An exception to the choice of voicings occurs in measure 2 of Rhy. Fill 1A where Sexton barres the 3rd, 4th and 5th strings at the 10th fret and hammers from G to A on the 5th string for a bit of bluesy melody against the underlying D5 harmony. Bramhall plays rhythm as Gtr. 1, including the accompanying heavy, dynamic fills under Sexton's vocals in Verse 2. In the following Chorus, to execute his unison bends, he pulls *down* on the 2nd string, 13th fret with the ring finger backed up by the middle while holding down the D note (1st string 10th fret) with the index. Conventional technique would call for pushing up on the 2nd string with either the ring or pinky finger with the index remaining on the 1st string. Observe how pulling down for bends provides Bramhall with an extra dose of expression bestowed only to those who play with guitars strung upside down.

MOONCHILD
Rory Gallagher

Rory Gallagher not only stands apart as one of the few notable Irish blues guitarists, but as one of the greats of any nationality. *Calling Card* (#163, 1976), his sixth release containing the energetic single, has been lauded as his best studio album. His too-early death in 1995 at age 47 was another tragic loss to the blues and rock community. He was a multi-talented player with a tremendous love and dedication to the blues.

TONE

Like Albert King, Albert Collins, and several others, Gallagher was literally identified with one instrument. His beloved, battered 1961 sunburst Strat – bought second hand in 1963 – was reputedly the first one imported into Ireland. Far from being committed to preserving his vintage prize, however, he modified it considerably over the years. The list includes tuners, nut, pickguard, 5-way selector switch and most importantly, neck and middle pickups from a '74 Strat along with a custom bridge pickup. Kent Armstrong apparently makes authentic pickup copies. A Vox AC-30 Top Boost or 1954 tweed Bassman amp, helped by a Hawk Treble Booster, were his hardware in the mid-seventies. A Strat through a Fender Deluxe Reverb or larger tube combo set "flat" with little or no reverb, along with the Hawk Treble Booster (which has been reissued by Flynn Amps as an RG signature model) will realistically approach his sound.

TECHNIQUE

Gallagher convinced his mother to spring for the £100 Strat by explaining how he would make and save money for the family by playing both rhythm and lead, negating the need for a second guitarist. The Intro highlights this ability as he weaves the melodic dyads of from the A minor scale with the steady pedal tone of the open A string via hybrid picking. Pay particular attention to the stunning lick in measures 11 and 12. Here he bends the D note (3rd string, 7th fret) with his ring finger up to E, vibratos, then taps the string with the edge of his pick, using the pick to fret the bent string at the 17th fret. Next he adds a bit of vibrato with his left hand, then quickly slides the pick from the 17th to the (theoretically) 24th fret before releasing the pick and the bend back to D: a sensational "trick" assumed not be heard until the late seventies and eighties by metal guitarists. Another cool lick is found in measures 11and 12 of the second Verse, where he rips a series of slippery triplet pull-offs.

ONE BOURBON, ONE SCOTCH, ONE BEER
George Thorogood

The ultimate "bar band" guitarist, George Thorogood came boogying out of Delaware in the mid-seventies where he had been a semi-pro baseball player. His debut album, *George Thorogood and the Destroyers* (1977), exposed a man and his band playing the music of Bo Diddley, Elmore James and John Lee Hooker, both simply and with raw, unrefined power. Those prime virtues of great blues-rock have been a major element of his ongoing popularity, outweighed only by his unparalleled enthusiasm.

TONE

Thorogood has been linked to one iconic guitar; the rather proletariat 1961-70 thinline Gibson ES-125 with two P-90 pickups. This axe plugged straight into a blackface Fender Bassman comprised his gear on his first album, and he has stuck with the same "budget," hollow body axe ever since. He currently uses GHS medium gauge strings. A Gibson ES-330 or Epiphone Casino on the bridge pickup into anything from a 15 to 40-watt tube combo will get the grit. Start with the volume and all tone controls on 10 and the guitar volume at 1 or 2 and work up (and down on the amp) from there.

TECHNIQUE

Thorogood tends to play basic country blues licks in E minor pentatonic scale positions with a standard Robert Johnson-type turnaround, albeit with much attitude. However, the more demanding skill in performing his music comes from his fingerpicking style. He cites Muddy Waters, Robert Johnson and even bluegrass guitarist Lester Flatt as influences, with Hound Dog Taylor as the most important. In the Intro he uses his index finger to pick upwards on strings 1 and 2 on the "off beats" while thumping the muted 6th string with his bare thumb on the downbeats to create the boogie rhythm. Be sure to form the open E major chord in case other strings are accidentally struck and to easily access the classic hammer-on from the minor 3rd (G) to the major 3rd (G♯) with the middle finger in measures 8 and 13. Check out how he frequently hits the open 6th string while simultaneously picking up on the open 1st and 2nd strings in a pinching motion with the thumb and index finger.

ONE WAY OUT
Allman Brothers Band

On October 29, 1971, Duane Allman was tragically killed in a motorcycle accident in the midst of recording the fourth Allman Brothers album, *Eat a Peach*. Despite the loss of their leader, the remaining members vowed to continue on in his memory. The album was released on February 12, 1972 (#4) as a double-disk set consisting of studio and live tracks left over from *Live at the Fillmore East* in March 1971, as well as from other concerts. "One Way Out" is from their final performance at the Fillmore in June, and was originally recorded by Elmore James in 1961. Duane was quoted as saying, perhaps in jest, "Elmore was a pretty good slide player, but he never did get to hear me play!"

TONE

Dickey Betts (Gtr. 1) played 100-watt Marshall 4x12 stacks with hi-fidelity JBL speakers, contributing to his generally "sweeter," cleaner sound. Duane Allman (Gtr. 2) used the smaller 50-watt model with 4x12 cabs containing Cerwin-Vega speakers, giving him a more aggressive, distorted tone, as he could push it harder without producing overwhelming volume. Betts played a '57 Gold Top Les Paul while Allman used his recently-acquired '59 LP Standard (nicknamed "Hot 'Lanta"). A Les Paul or other quality solid body guitar with humbuckers set on the neck (Intro, Verses) or bridge "pup" (Guitar Solos) through a Marshall, or other high gain tube amp – adjusted according to which guitar tone one is trying to replicate – should get the vibe.

TECHNIQUE

Allman (Gtr. 2 – open E tuning) used bare right hand fingers and wore his glass Coricidin bottle slider on his middle finger. It is usually recommended to wear the slide on the pinky finger in the manner of solo prewar country blues guitarists in order to more easily access chord forms. Nonetheless, his choice of finger actually allowed him to better back Betts (Gtr. 1) in the first Guitar Solo, as Allman's rhythm licks require fretting notes with the index, ring and pinky fingers. Observe that both guitarists switch to their bridge pickups and peg their volume controls when soloing.

PEACE PIPE
Cry of Love

Cry of Love, formed in North Carolina in 1989 with guitarist Audley Freed, created classic hard rock similar to Bad Company and Lynyrd Skynyrd. Their debut, *Brother* (#13 Heatseekers,1993) contained "Peace Pipe" (#1 Mainstream Rock Tracks), a lament for Native Americans. Their only other album was *Diamonds & Debris* from 1997. Later that year they disbanded. Freed would next play with the Black Crowes from 1998-2001.

TONE

Freed reportedly played through a Marshall Silver Jubilee, a 1973 JMP Superlead with added master volume, a TS-9 Tube Screamer and Vox wah. A blue Warmoth hard tail strat copy with a Duncan JB Jr. stacked humbucker in the bridge position was his axe. The official video shows him with a white hard tail Strat sporting a left-handed neck with a double-coil humbucker in the bridge position, set on the middle single-coil. As on other tracks featuring a Strat/Marshall stack combination, the iconic guitar is a necessity but a smaller (and cheaper) Marshall combo or a high gain Fender or boutique amp running hot should produce the desired punch. In lieu of swapping a humbucker into your favorite Strat, however, a TS-9 (or TS-8 or even a newer TS-7) Tube Screamer will provide extra overdrive power.

TECHNIQUE

The ultra cool guitar hook in Riff A, first heard in the Intro and then driving the Verses, may prove more challenging than it first might seem. It's important to leave the index finger at the 2nd fret as a barre throughout the playing of the riff. The picking direction is paramount for the necessary speed. Pick downwards for the initial power chord and the B note that follows. Then pick upwards on the A, down on the E (hammer on to F♯) and up on the A. For the vibrated double stops in measures 2 and 5 of the Pre-Chorus, use your middle and ring fingers on the 9th fret of the 3rd and 4th strings respectively. Pull the strings downwards, using the first knuckle area of your index finger as a fulcrum against the bottom edge of the fretboard.

ROCK N ROLL SUSIE
Pat Travers

As a youngster, the veteran Canadian rocking blues guitarist saw Hendrix in Ottawa and has been cranking bare-knuckles blues and rock since before his official debut in 1976. He has garnered the respect of his peers, but deserves more reward than his commercially checkered career has provided. His sophomore outing *Makin' Magic* (1977), with the single "Rock n Roll Susie," considerably ratcheted up the "heavy" quotient, and is beloved by his loyal fans who take the album title literally.

TONE

Travers turned the trick of making a double cutaway 1965 Gibson Melody Maker – refitted with two humbuckers to replace the "special" single coils – his iconic guitar. Since then, Gibson made him a custom, double cutaway Les Paul. In the late seventies he also used a '73 Tele to record. A 50-watt Marshall and an early master volume 100-watter, augmented with an MXR Phase 90, MXR Blue Box and Vox wah were the essence of his massive recorded and live sound; that, along with playing loud! A Marshall tube combo or larger amp with a humbucking-powered solid body on the bridge pickup played at inconsiderate volume for the neighbors would be the ultimate way to play like Travers. However, any quality, high gain, 40 to 50-watt tube combo with the bass boosted to speaker-testing levels should produce the necessary thunder.

TECHNIQUE

Travers rips on a bruising boogie number vaguely reminiscent of Boston's "Rock & Roll Band," as well similar to "boogie chillen" themes in the air in the seventies. Still the signature open A chord riff, anchored by the index finger at the 2nd fret, swings hard while Travers inserts subtle variations to keep it from sounding mechanical. Know that he was leading a power trio at this time, and thereby plays all guitar parts. This is long before second guitarist Pat Thrall was brought in. Consequently, one must choose the main guitar parts such as Gtr. 1 in Riff A1 of the Intro, and Gtr. 1 in measures 11–13 of the Interlude. Also be aware how the half-step dip on G5 in the next to last measure of the Guitar Solo was accomplished by pushing forward on the neck of the slender Melody Maker while holding the body tightly with the elbow. Note: Proceed with caution!

SWLABR
Cream

Psychedelic lyrics meet romping blues-rock in an adrenaline rush just as powerful as it was in 1967 when it appeared on *Disraeli Gears* (#4) and as the "B" side of the single "Sunshine of Your Love" (#5). Cream enacted a paradigm shift with their second album as their progressive, creative approach to interpreting blues forms, along with the virtuosic chops and thrilling tone – of Eric Clapton in particular – had a huge effect on rock music. BTW: The song title is an acronym for "She Walks Like a Bearded Rainbow."

TONE
Everyone involved in the recording sessions, including Ahmet Ertegun from Atlantic Records, recalls how incredibly loud Cream was in the studio. Clapton appears to have played a '58–60 triple-pickup Les Paul Custom on the middle pickup for rhythm, and his famous "The Fool" '64 Gibson SG with early "patent" humbuckers for the solo through a 50-watt Marshall half stack containing four 25-watt Celestion greenbacks with all EQ controls jacked up. The secret to his unique lead tone on the track (and others on the album) is his "Woman Tone" acquired by playing on the bridge pickup with the tone control rolled all the way off, and the guitar volume adjusted as high as needed. A solid body humbucking equipped axe – set as prescribed above – plugged straight into a high gain Marshall or similar combo with the controls (except for reverb) floored, should produce a reasonable facsimile of the lead sound.

TECHNIQUE
In the Intro, fret the E chord with the ring, pinky, and middle fingers (low to high) as if it were a barre chord but without the index finger. This will make the transition up the neck to the G and A chords more efficient. Additionally, release the pressure off the fretted notes after each strum in measures 1 and 3 to create the syncopated, staccato effect. Approach the E chord in Rhy. Fig. 1 with the same fingering as the Intro, while accessing the fretted notes of the Bm9 with the ring and index fingers (low to high).

TRAVELING RIVERSIDE BLUES
Led Zeppelin

Though there was a bit of overlap chronologically, Led Zeppelin could be seen as the next evolution of heavy British blues-rock following Cream, despite major differences in material and style. "Truth" be told, Jeff Beck felt Jimmy Page ripped off the idea for Zep from his first solo album upon leaving the Yardbirds. Recorded in the spring and early summer of 1969 and including the Robert Johnson classic, the oft-bootlegged *Led Zeppelin: BBC Sessions* (#12) would go 2x Platinum when released in 1997, and were the first live tracks from the band in 21 years – 17 years after pulling the plug on the band following the accidental death of drummer John Bonham.

TONE
It seems likely Page played the slide accompaniment on his black 1967 Vox Phantom XII 12-string solid body electric; the same guitar he played with the Yardbirds on "Little Games" as well as on "Thank You" on *Led Zeppelin II*. For the overdubbed Guitar Solo, it sounds like Jimmy enlisted his '59 Telecaster, a gift from Beck, possibly through a Vox AC-30 Top Boost. He may have stepped on a stomp box like a Sola Sound Tone Bender MkII, also popular with JB at the time. A 12-string acoustic or electric is required for the slide, as is a Telecaster or a Strat on the bridge pickup for the solo pumped through a 20 to 40-watt tube combo with a Tube Screamer or similar distortion box.

TECHNIQUE
Page wears his metal slider on his ring finger, though the pinky is always recommended in order to free the first three fingers for fretting. For the descending, open string turnaround patterns without the slide, the left-hand index finger could be used to fret each note while the right hand employs hybrid picking. Observe how in measures 3 (last two notes) and 4 of the Intro just the pick and right-hand index finger would suffice, while the left-hand ring and middle fingers could be used to fret in measure 5. However, in measures 7, 9, 11 and 13, utilize the pick in conjunction with the right-hand index and middle fingers. For the fretted chords and double-stops throughout, use whatever combination of left-hand index, middle, and ring fingers (if the slide is on the pinky) is most comfortable, as there are different efficient options available due to the open tuning. BTW: As the Guitar Solo is an overdub without the slide, standard fingerings apply, as much as "standard" could be said to describe Page in full Zep flight in measures 11 and 12!

TRUE LIES
Kenny Wayne Shepherd

Born Kenny Wayne Brobst, the young phenom promoted his three names to make the connection to his idol and main inspiration, Stevie Ray Vaughan. *Trouble Is…* (#74, 1997), his second release, went Platinum, and featured the Mainstream Rock Tracks hits "Blue on Black" (#1), "Slow Ride" (#3) and "Somehow, Somewhere, Someway" (#3). In 2007 his blues cred got a boost when he toured the US jamming with a selection of blues luminaries and released as the CD/DVD set *10 Days Out: Blues from the Backroads*. In addition, in 2011 he recorded *Live in Chicago* with Hubert Sumlin, Willie "Big Eyes" Smith and Pinetop Perkins.

TONE

Shepherd has been playing and recording with a 1961 sunburst, rosewood neck Strat since he was 17, strung with brawny .012–.058 gauges. His main studio amp was 1964 Fender blackface Vibroverb enhanced with either a vintage TS-8 or TS-9 Tube Screamer. Get his classic post-SRV, blues-rock tone by setting the Strat selector switch in the out-of-phase notch between the middle and bridge pickup. Plug into a 20 to 50-watt tube combo amp with the volume near max, treble at 6, middle at 5, bass at 4, and reverb at 4. The Tube Screamer should be used more as a preamp via turning the level higher than the drive.

TECHNIQUE

Proper technique for playing the signature Riff A is as follows: Use your left hand middle finger for the pair of hammer-ons on the 4th string. For the last two fretted notes in beat 2, use your middle and index fingers respectively. Bend the G with your ring finger by pulling up one-quarter step to the "true blue note," located between the flatted 3rd and major 3rd. Shepherd teaches a lesson from "Trio Blues Guitar 101" in the Guitar Solo as, for each of the two times the G to A chords come around, he defines the major tonality with appropriate chordal forms, including propulsive ascending harmony in 6ths relative to each change in measures 21 and 22.

TWICE AS HARD
Black Crowes

What Guns n' Roses were to hard rock in the late eighties, the Black Crowes were to hard blues-rock in the nineties (although the former had a much longer shelf life). Their debut album, *Shake Your Money Maker* (#4, 1990) – named for an Elmore James blues classic – went 3x Platinum and contained "Twice as Hard" (#11), plus a pair of #1 Mainstream Rock Tracks singles "Hard to Handle" and "She Talks to Angels." It is their only album with second guitarist Jeff Cease, as the Robinson brothers defiantly stuck to their musical choice despite changing trends.

TONE

In the Crowes, Rich Robinson at first played a '68 Les Paul Deluxe Gold Top, a circa '72 Fender Deluxe, and a '68 Tele with a humbucker swapped into the neck position. The latter instrument, which he fondly nicknamed "Moneymaker," appears on this track, set on the 'Bucker and played with a brass slide through a Marshall Silver Jubilee amp. A Tele Deluxe with two humbuckers (or a Custom with one in the neck position) would be your best choice of guitars, as they impart that all-important "twang" along with high output. A 50-watt or bigger high gain tube amp cranked, or in conjunction with a stomp box, completes the aggressive sound.

TECHNIQUE

Affirming the prewar country blues guitar maxim that "it is best to wear the slider on the pinky finger," Robinson plays fretted C5 and F/C voicings alá Keith Richards in the Pre-Chorus with his index, middle, and ring fingers, while the slide resides in place. Cease often doubles Robinson's slide licks, but without the slide.

WALKING THROUGH THE PARK
Gary Moore

As the "other" great Irish blues-rocker (see "Moonchild"), Gary Moore was established as a hard rock and fusion guitarist in Thin Lizzy and other projects before following his muse and releasing *Still Got the Blues* (#83, 1990), which featured Albert King and Albert Collins. He went on to record ten more blues-based albums, including his last studio disk, *Bad for You, Baby* (2008), before his tragic death by heart attack in 2011.

TONE

Though famous through association for once being the owner of Peter Green's iconic '59 'Burst, Moore played a '68 Tele through a 1989 reissue of the '62 Fender brown tolex Vibroverb on this classic Muddy Waters tune. The pedals on this track include both the T-Rex Moller boost/overdrive and the T-Rex Mudhoney distortion/overdrive. The thick gain, or nasty bite, indicate the presence of one or the other. To get his crunchy vibe, try a Tele on the bridge pickup through a Fender or similar 20 to 40-watt combo goosed by a high gain stomp box.

TECHNIQUE

As the guitarist in a trio recording sans overdubs, Moore fills the sonic space with snarling tone and by fattening up the signature licks in the Intro while playing with the same overdriven tone throughout. Where the original (1958) had Little Walter blowing single-note lines in unison with pianist Otis Spann, Moore inserts dyads in 3rds into the I, IV and V changes. The concept and technique of playing out of moveable minor or major pentatonic boxes is inimical to classic blues guitar forms.

Be Careful with a Fool

Words and Music by B.B. King and Joe Bihari

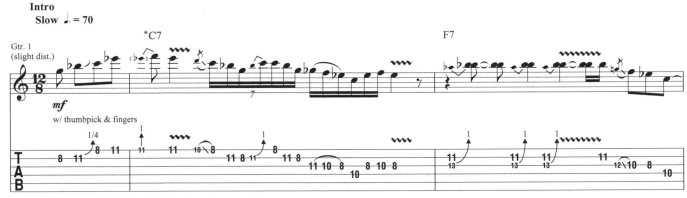

*Chord symbols reflect overall harmony.

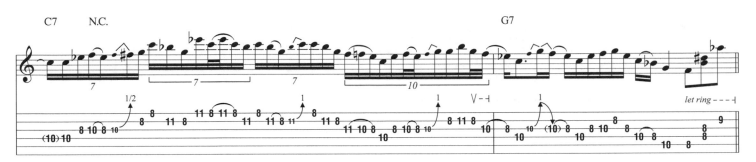

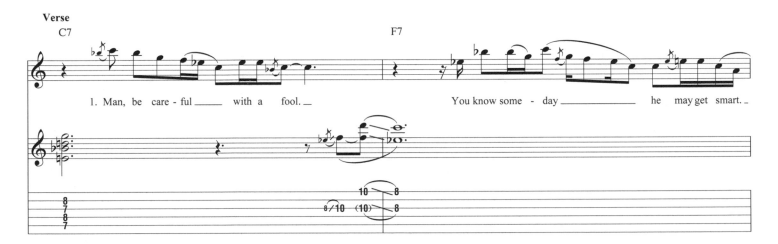

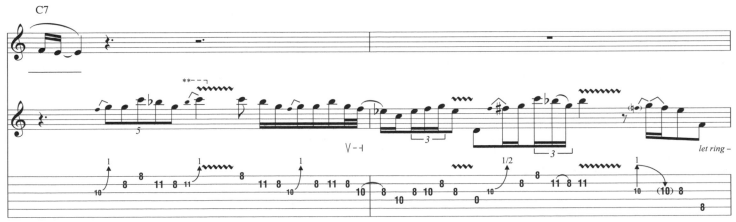

**Played behind the beat.

The way I used to love you, ba - by, ___   how   bad ___ it's gon-na

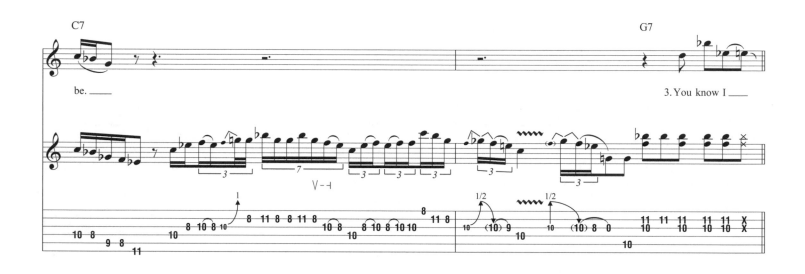

be. ___   3. You know I ___

Verse

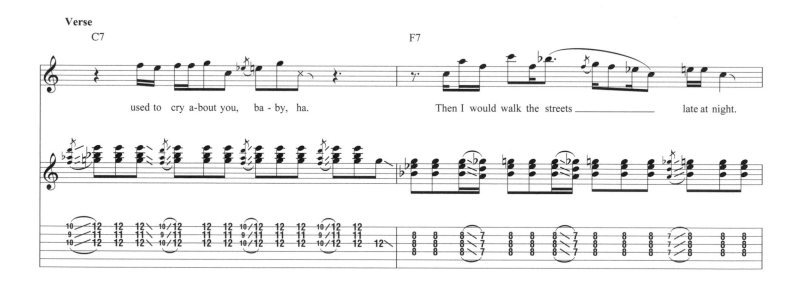

used to   cry a-bout you,   ba - by, ha.   Then I would walk the streets ___ late at night.

Guitar Solo

Oh, yeah.

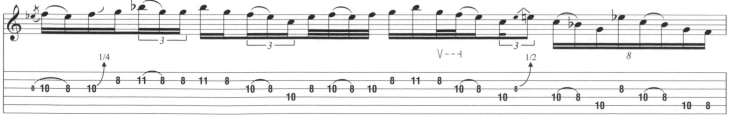

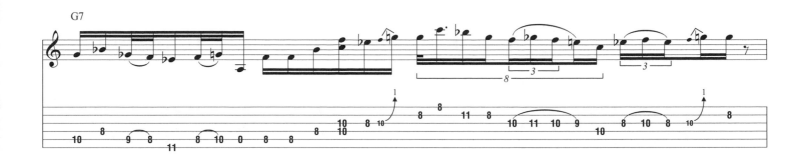

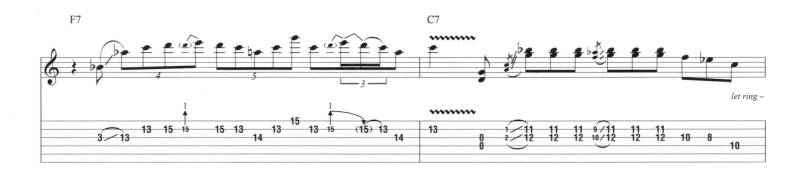

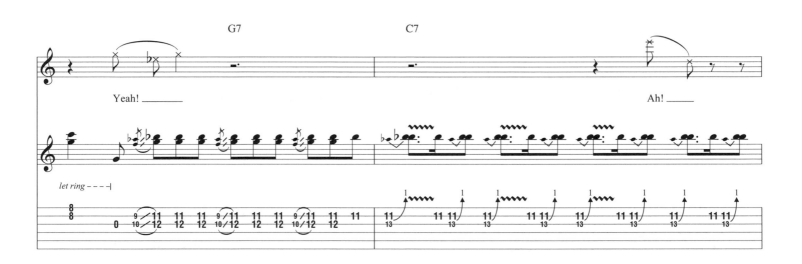

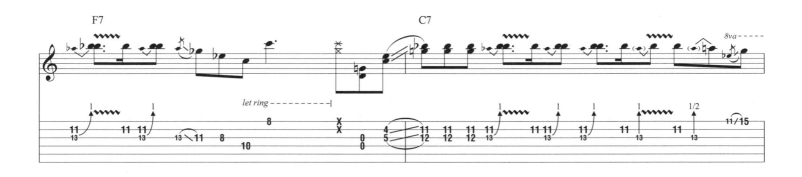

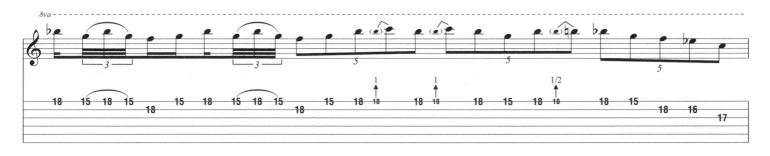

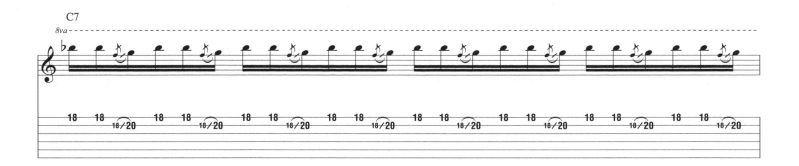

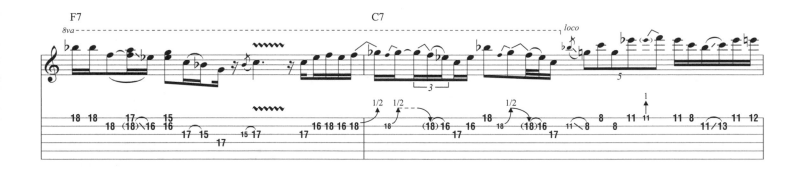

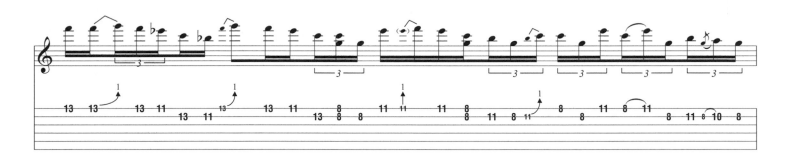

F7

Yeah, ba - by.

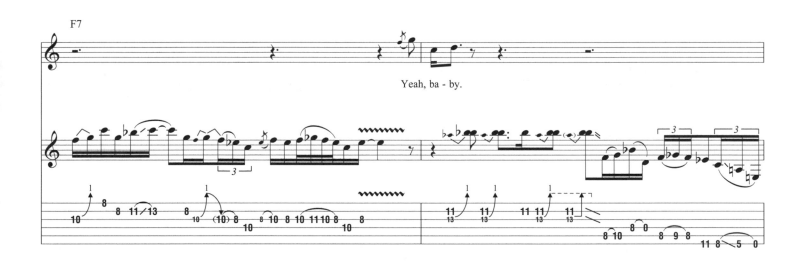

C7

Pitch: G
*Refers to 3rd string only.

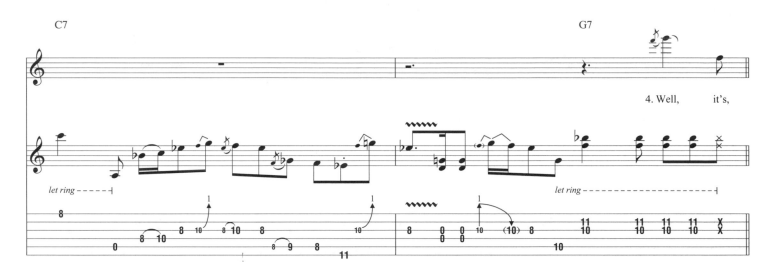

4. Well, it's,

uh, fi - n'ly o - ver, ba - by.   Whoa, __ I be-lieve _____ this is __ the end, __ ah,

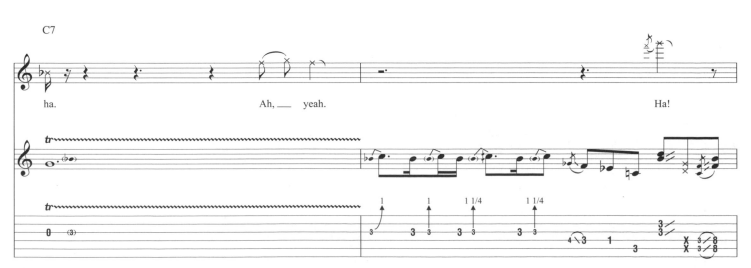

ha.   Ah, __ yeah.   Ha!

from The Paul Butterfield Blues Band - *The Paul Butterfield Blues Band*

Born in Chicago

Words and Music by Nick Gravenites

1. I was born __

Verse

Gtr. 2: w/ Rhy. Fig. 1

__ in Chi - ca - go   in nine-teen and for - ty one. __   I was born __

__ in Chi - ca - go   in nine-teen and for - ty one. __   Well, my

3. Well, my

Verse

sec-ond friend went down when I was twen-ty one years of age.

Well, my

sec-ond friend went down when I was twen-ty one years of age.

Well, there's

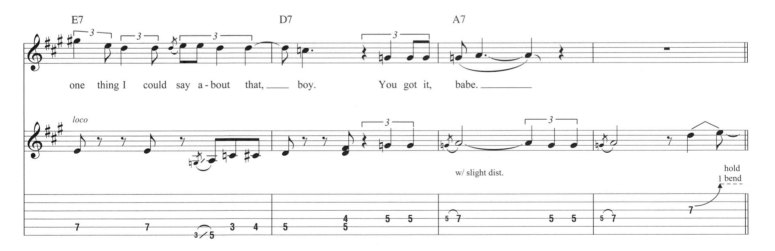

one thing I could say a-bout that, boy. You got it, babe.

Guitar Solo

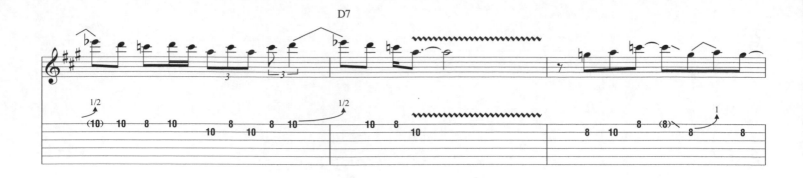

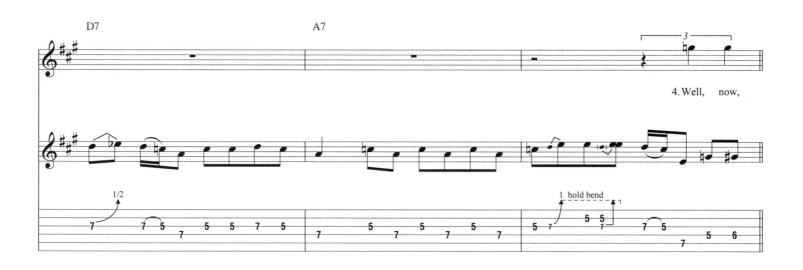

4. Well, now,

Verse

Gtr. 2: w/ Rhy. Fig. 1

rules are all right __ if there's some-one left to play the game.   Well, now,

P.M.

*w/ wah-wah

*Wah-wah in open (toe up) position.

32

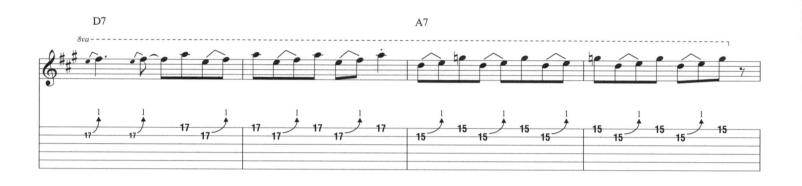

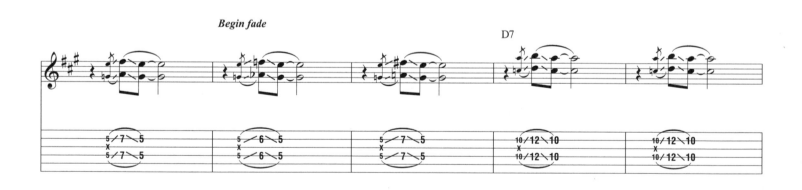

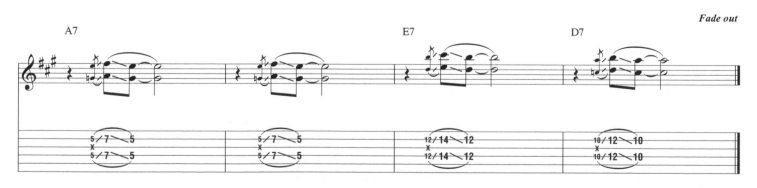

from Robin Trower - *Bridge of Sighs*

Bridge of Sighs

Words and Music by Robin Trower

Intro
Slowly ♩ = 48

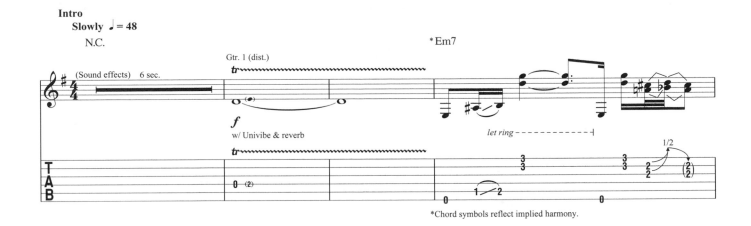

*Chord symbols reflect implied harmony.

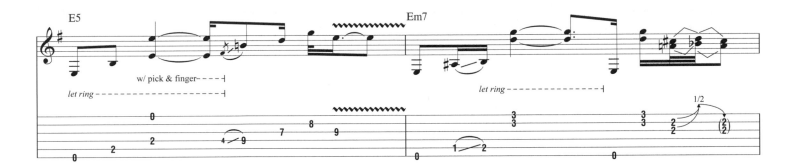

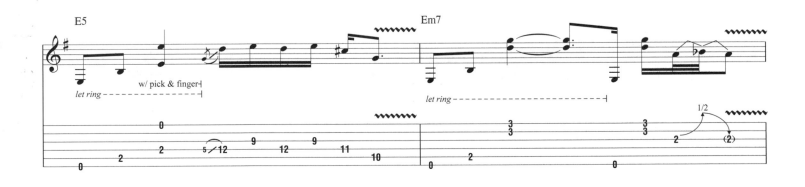

Verse

* Played ahead of the beat.

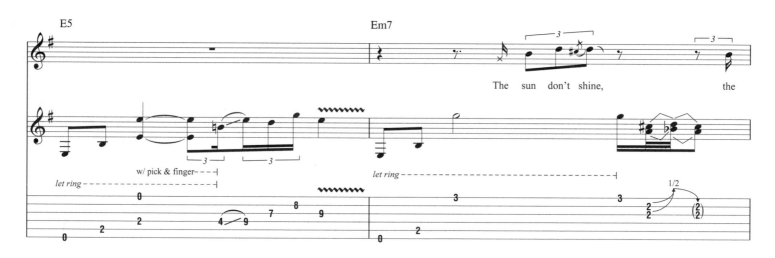

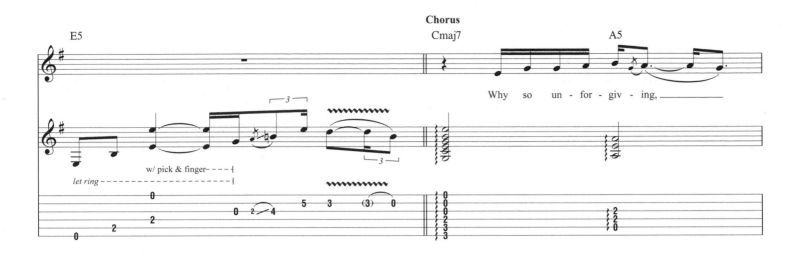

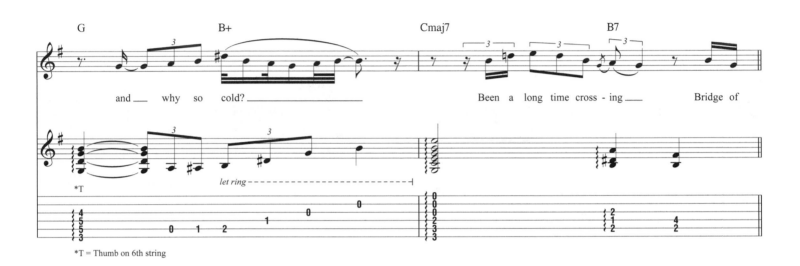

*T = Thumb on 6th string

Interlude

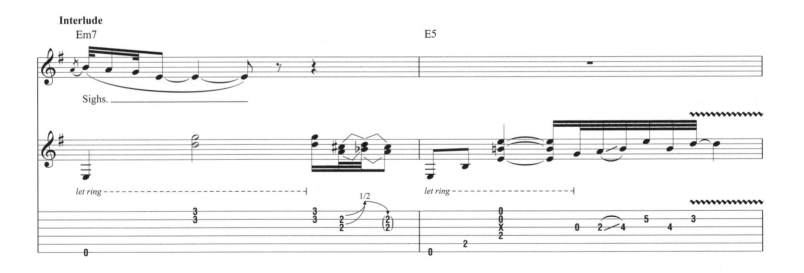

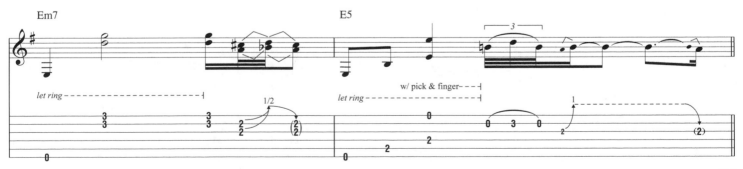

Verse

2. Cold wind blows, __ the Gods look down __ in an - ger on __ this poor child.

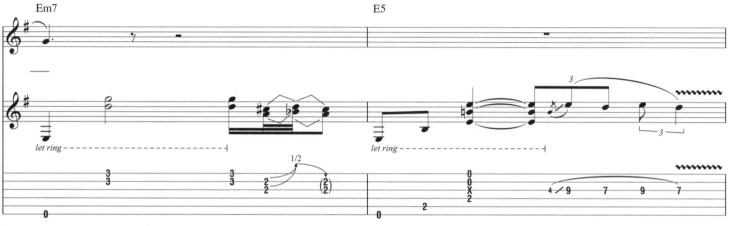

Cold wind blows, _____ the Gods look down __ in an - ger on this poor __

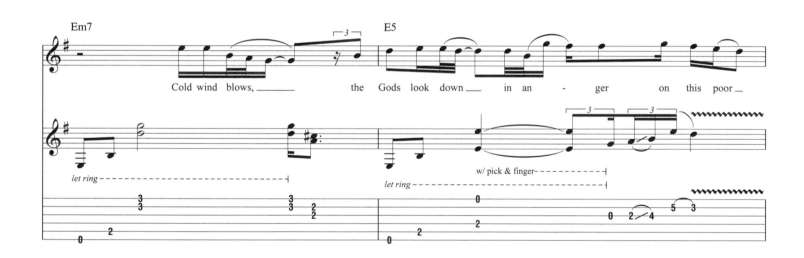

child. _____

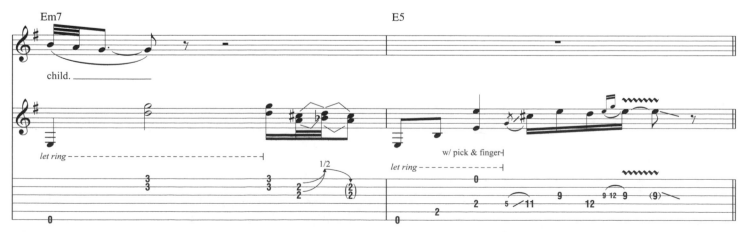

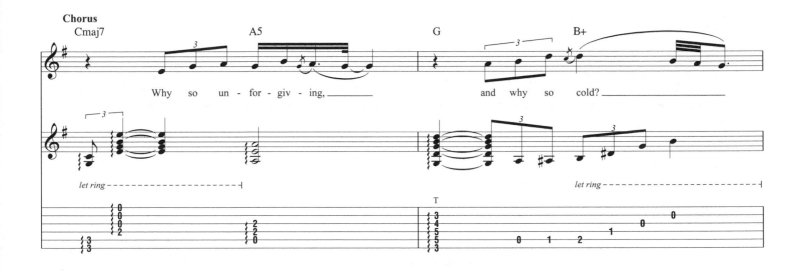

Chorus

Why so un-for-giv-ing, _____ and why so cold? _____

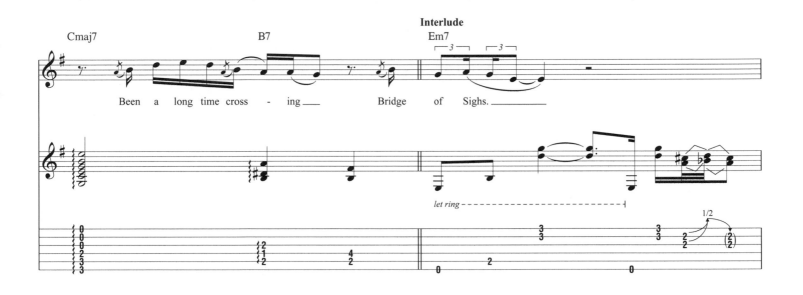

Interlude

Been a long time cross - ing _____ Bridge of Sighs.

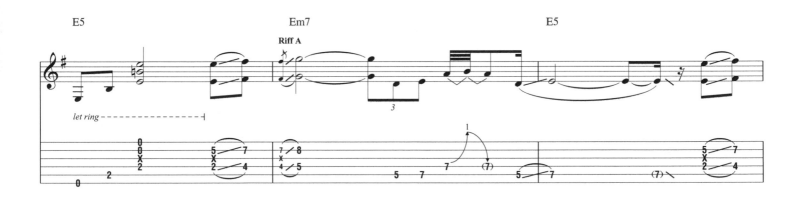

Riff A

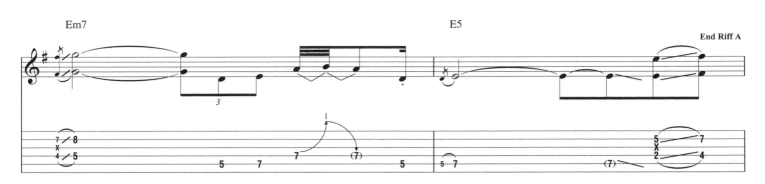

End Riff A

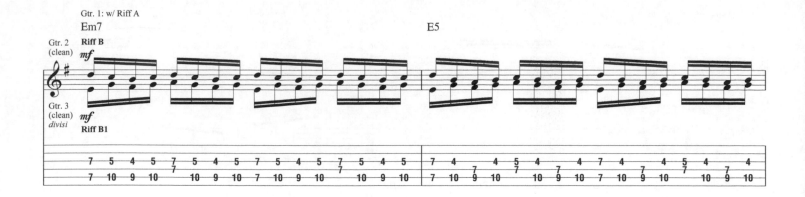

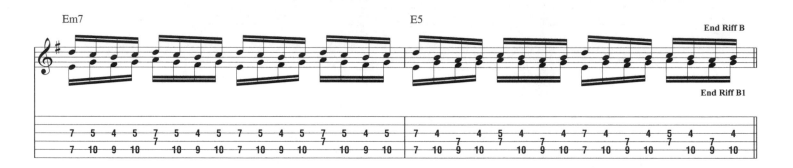

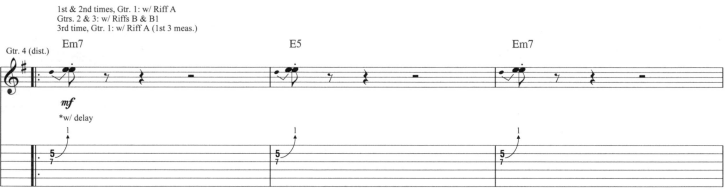

*Set delay for eighth-note regeneration w/ 7 repeats.

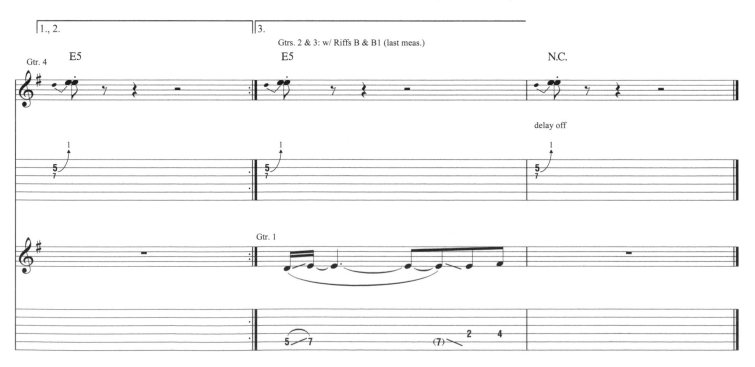

Broke Down on the Brazos

Words and Music by Warren Haynes, Matthew Abts, Daniel Louis and Jorgen Carlsson

Verse

Gtr. 4 tacet
2nd time, Gtr. 1: w/ Rhy. Fig. 2

Gtr. 2 tacet

F5

Fm7

1. Sur - round - ed by stran - gers; ___
3. Liv - ing in a dream, ___

(Play 1st time only)

Interlude

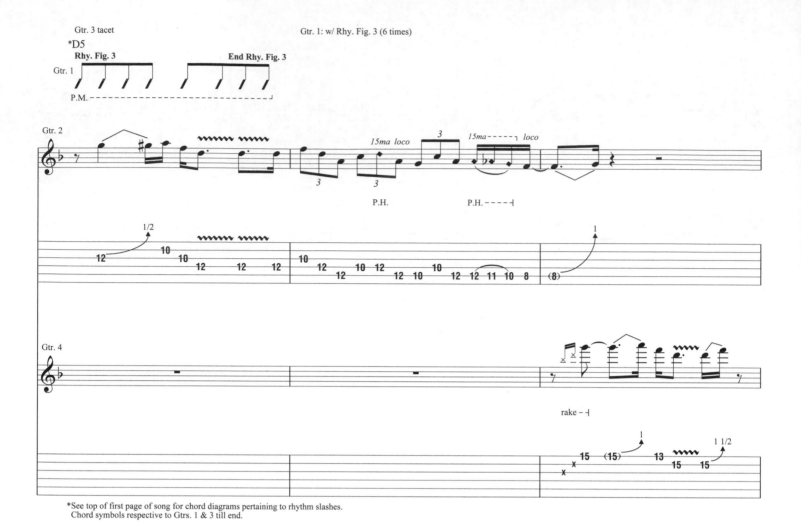

*See top of first page of song for chord diagrams pertaining to rhythm slashes.
Chord symbols respective to Gtrs. 1 & 3 till end.

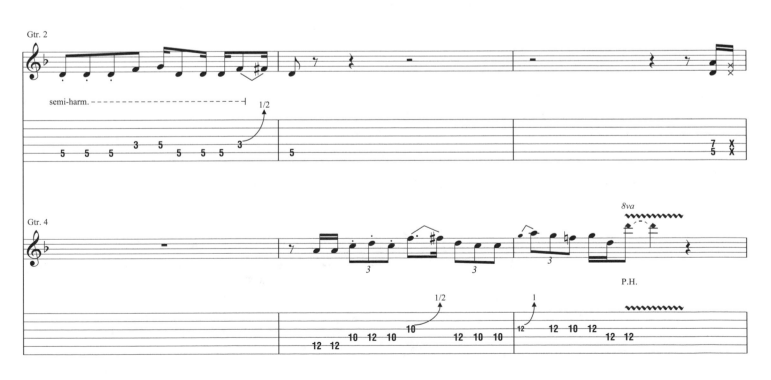

Gtrs. 1 & 3: w/ Riffs G & G1   Gtr. 1: w/ Rhy. Fig. 3 (7 times)

N.C.(Dm7)   E♭5   D5

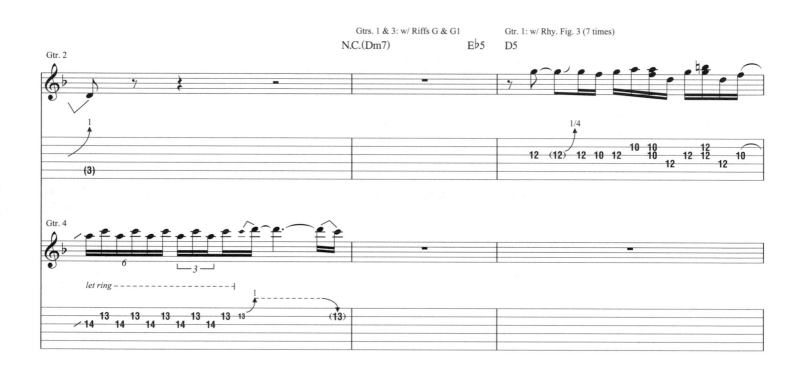

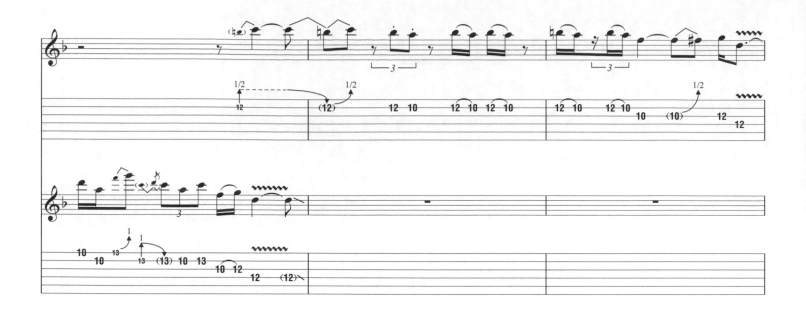

Gtrs. 1 & 3: w/ Riffs G & G1

N.C.(Dm7)   E♭5

Gtrs. 1 & 3

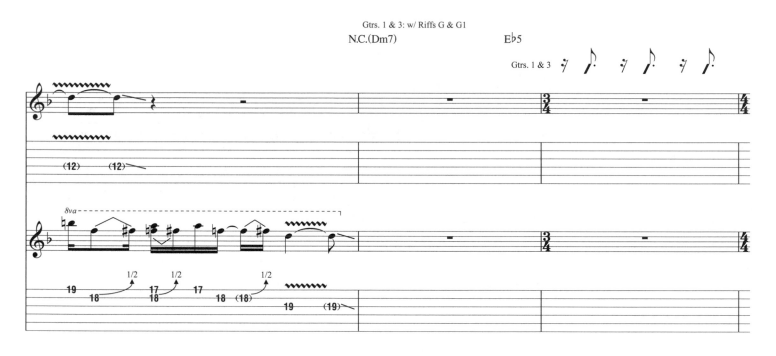

Gtr. 1: w/ Rhy. Fig. 3 (7 times)
Gtr. 3 tacet

D5

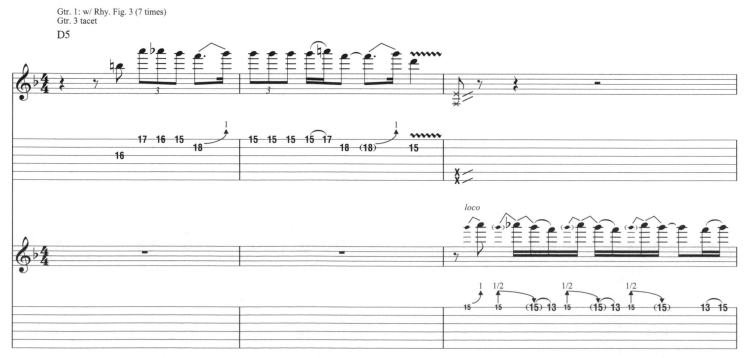

loco

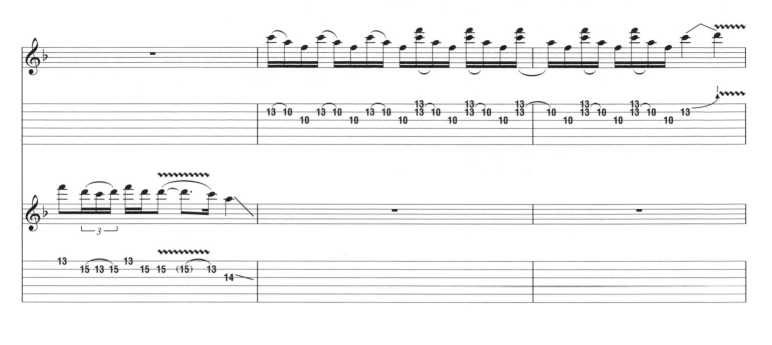

Gtrs. 1 & 3: w/ Riffs G & G1

N.C.(Dm7)　　　　　　Eb5

Gtrs. 1 & 3

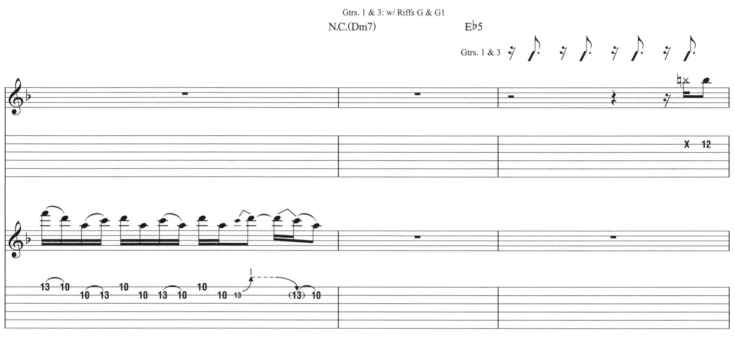

Gtr. 1: w/ Rhy. Fig. 3 (7 times)
Gtr. 3 tacet

Begin fade

D5

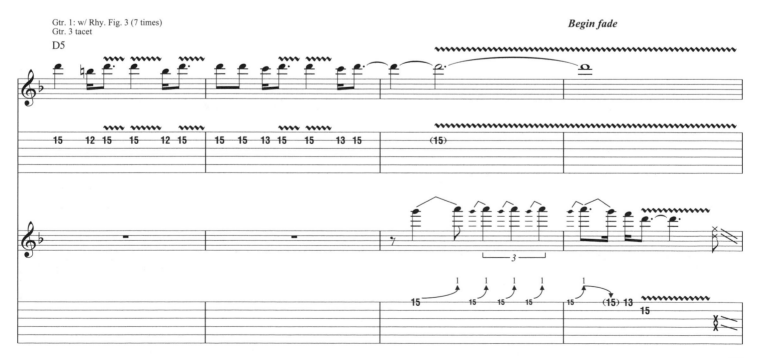

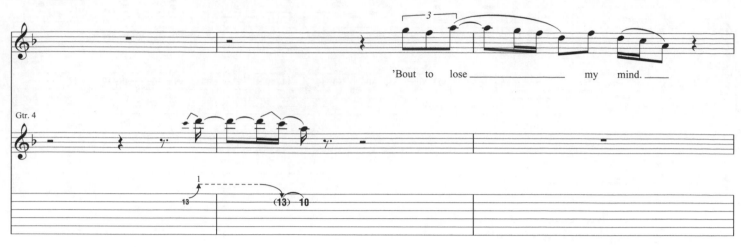

'Bout to lose _____ my mind. _____

Gtr. 1 & 3: w/ Riffs G & G1
Gtr. 4 tacet

N.C.(Dm7)　　　　　　　Eb5

Gtrs. 1 & 3

Fade out

Gtr. 1: w/ Rhy. Fig. 3 (4 times)
Gtr. 3 tacet

D5

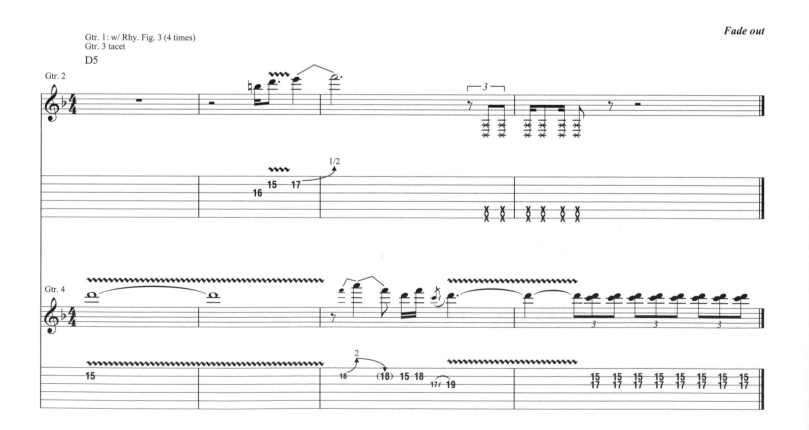

Come On, Pt. 1

Words and Music by Earl King

* Chord symbols reflect overall tonality.

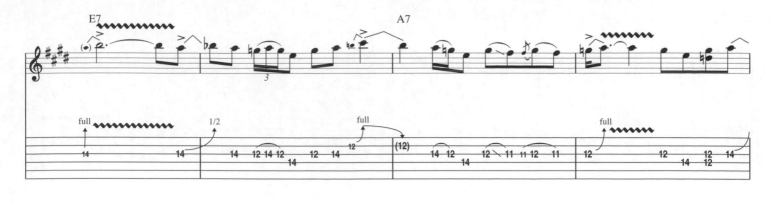

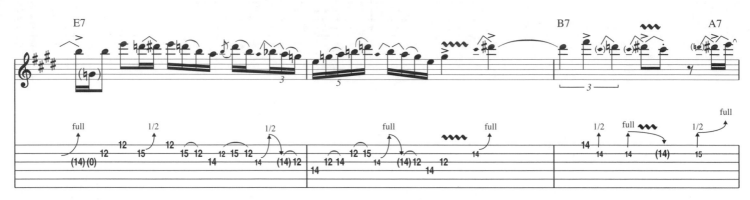

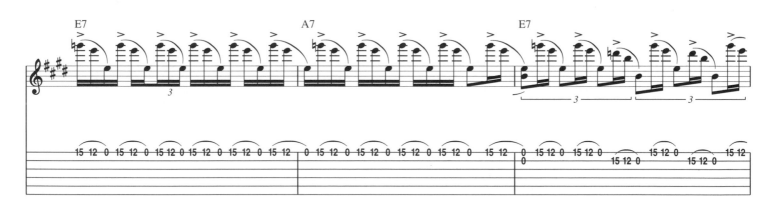

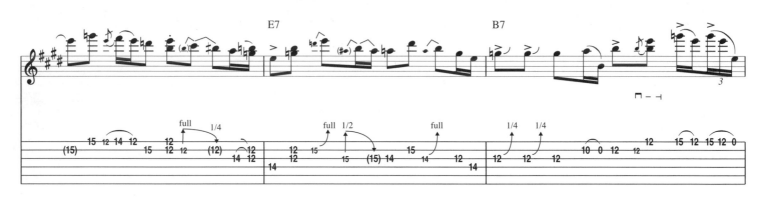

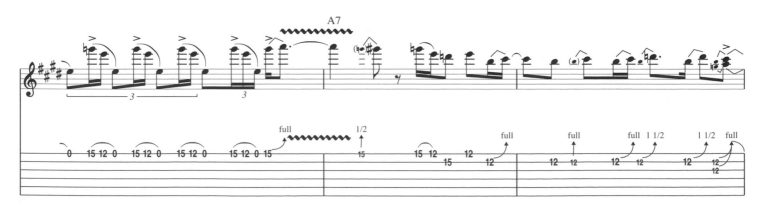

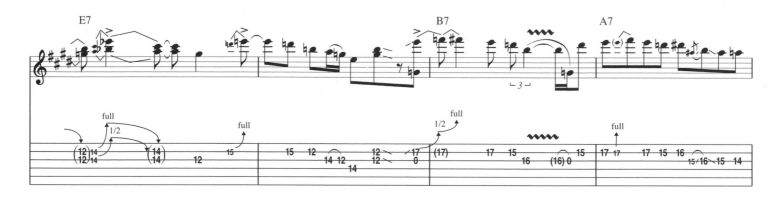

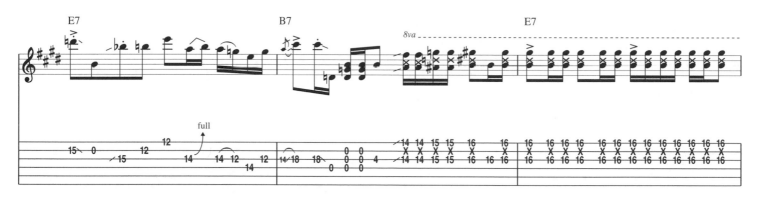

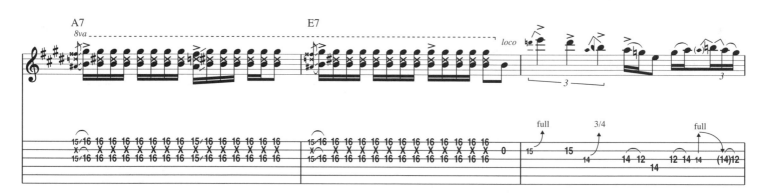

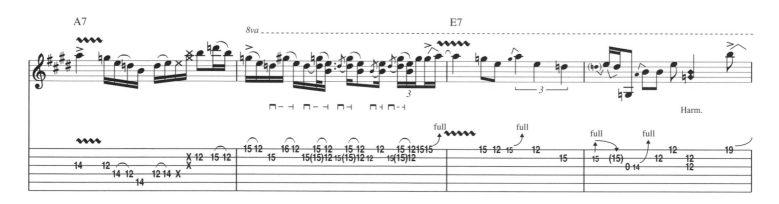

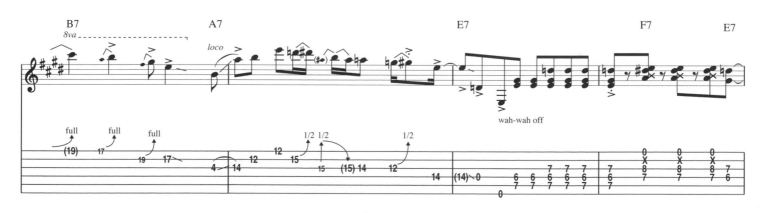

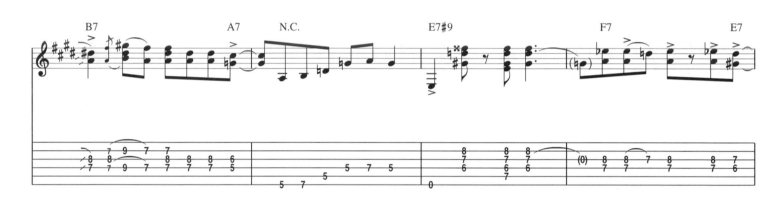

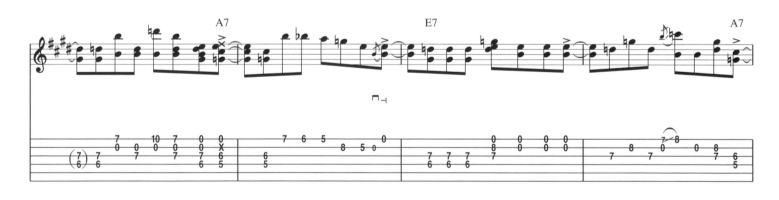

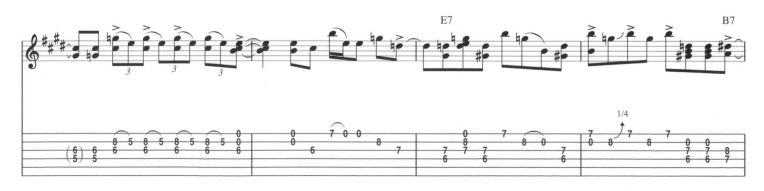

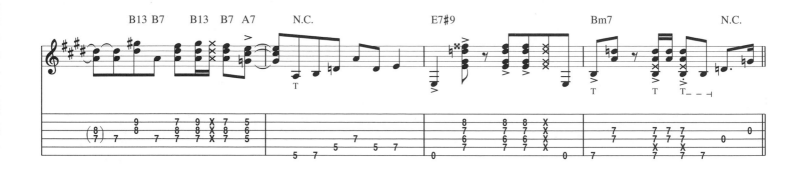

Verse

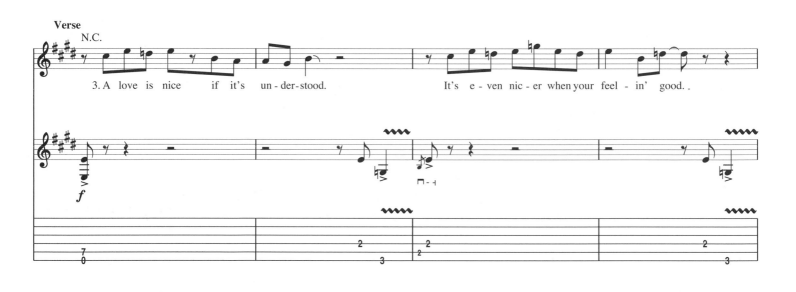

3. A love is nice   if it's un-der-stood.   It's e - ven nic - er when your feel - in' good.

You got me flip-pin' like a   flag on a pole, _   come on   sug - ar, let the good times   roll. _

Chorus

Hey!   Yeah, _   oh, let the good times   roll. _____   Hey! _

Thrill me ba - by, show pa-pa how good times roll. _ Oh,

ma-ma let me thrill your soul. _ Hey, _ let the good times roll.

Outro-Guitar Solo

Crossfire

Written by Bill Carter, Ruth Ellsworth, Reese Wynans, Tommy Shannon and Chris Layton

Tune down 1/2 step:
(low to high) E♭-A♭-D♭-G♭-B♭-E♭

Intro
Moderately ♩ = 112

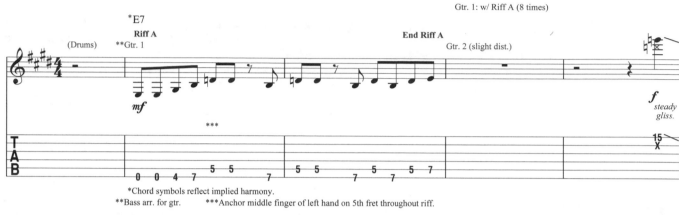

*Chord symbols reflect implied harmony.
**Bass arr. for gtr.   ***Anchor middle finger of left hand on 5th fret throughout riff.

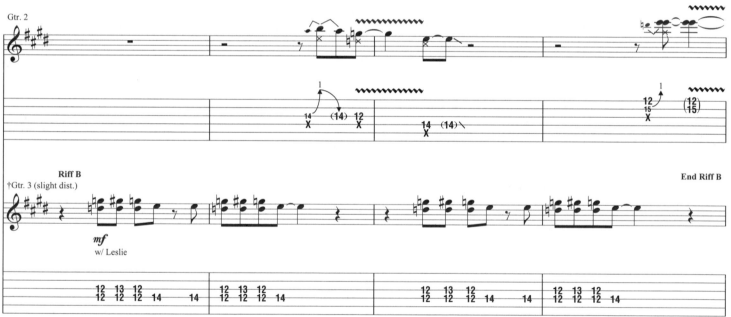

†Organ arr. for gtr.

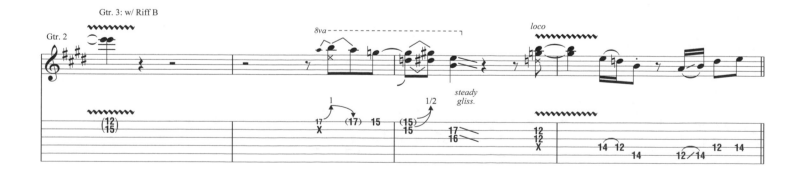

*Played behind the beat.

3. Save the strong, lose the weak, _ nev - er turn-ing the oth - er cheek. _

Strand-ed, _____ caught in ____ the cross - fire. Help me!

Outro-Guitar Solo

E7

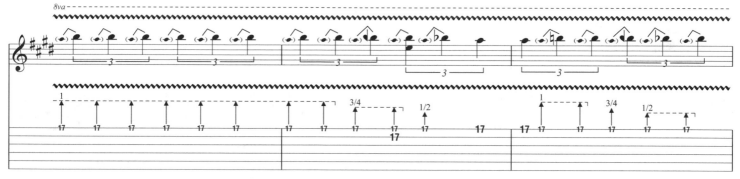

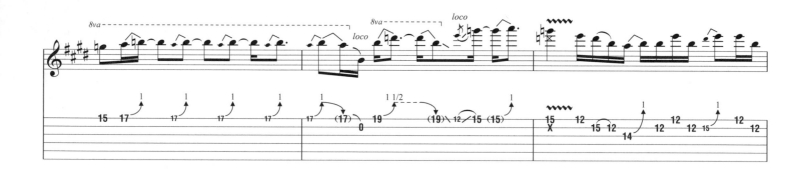

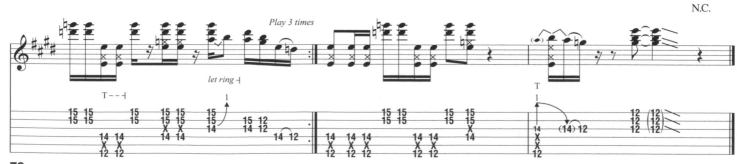

Going Down

Words and Music by Don Nix

Intro
Moderately slow ♩ = 88

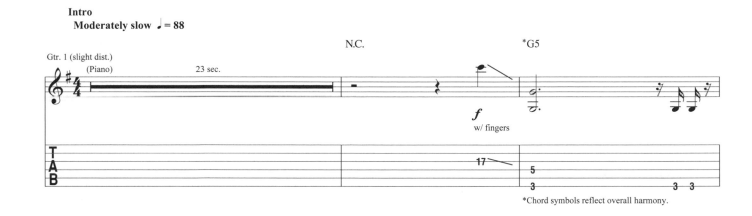

*Chord symbols reflect overall harmony.

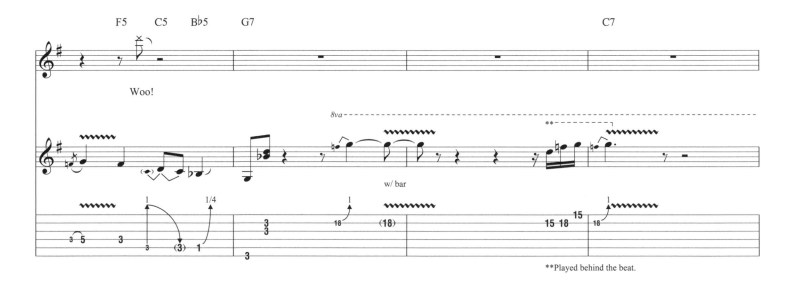

**Played behind the beat.

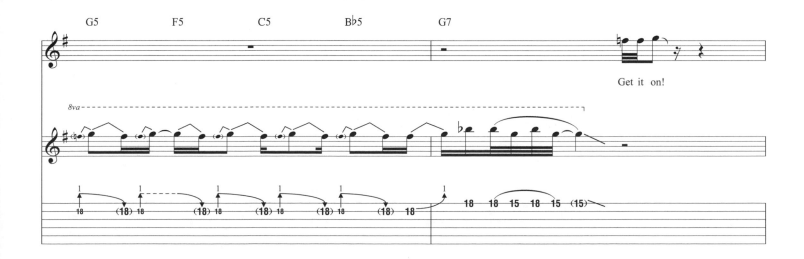

*Played behind the beat.

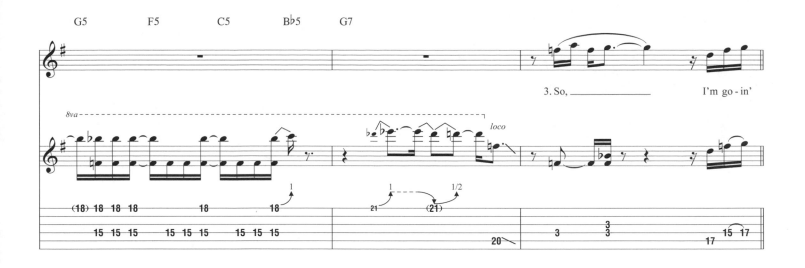

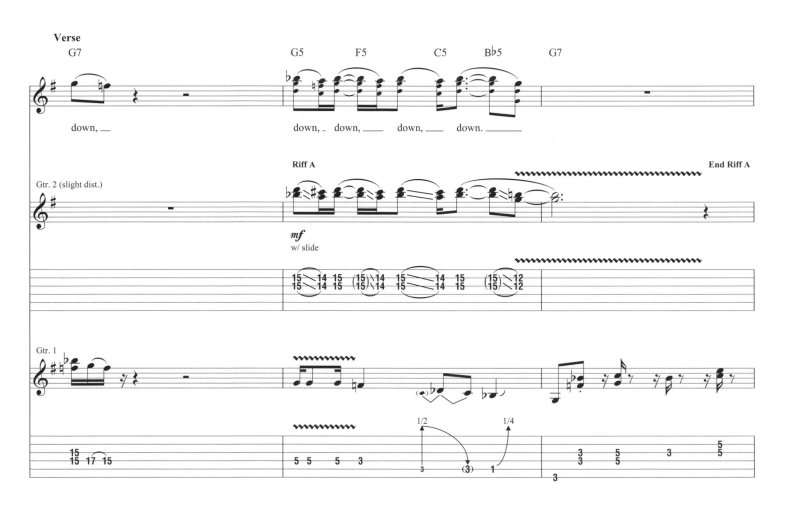

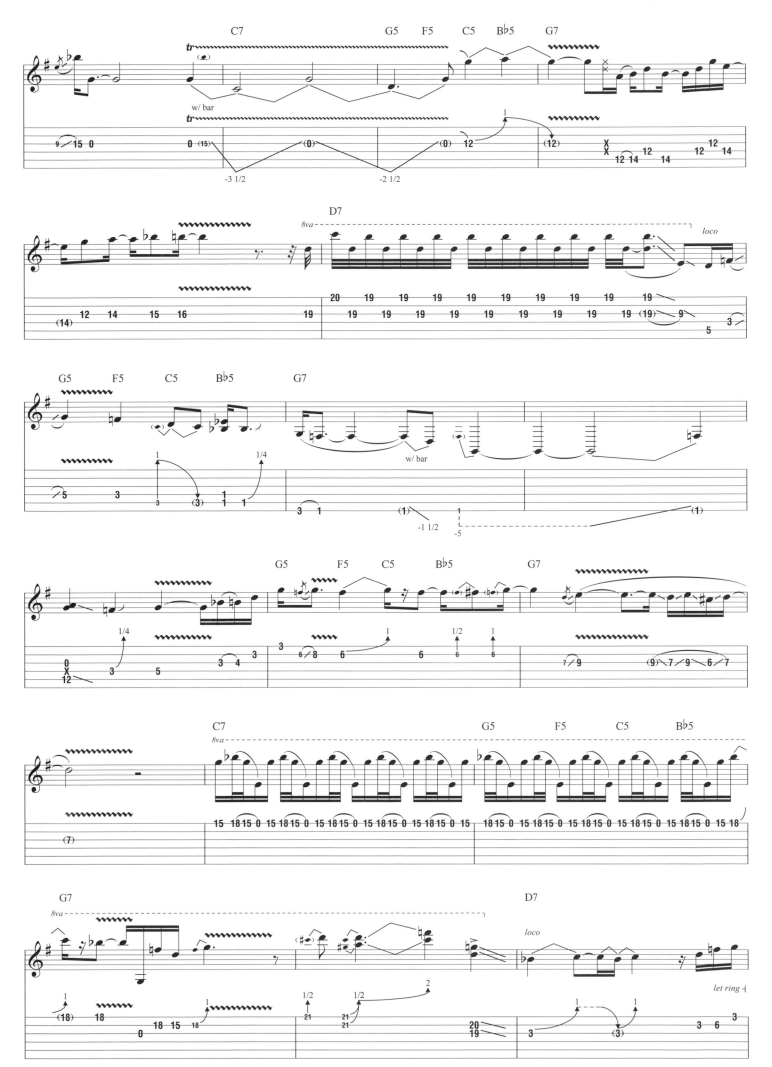

*Decrease to 1/2 volume.   **Swell to full volume.

Going Up the Country

Words and Music by Alan Wilson

Gtr. 1: Capo VIII

Intro
Fast ♩ = 163

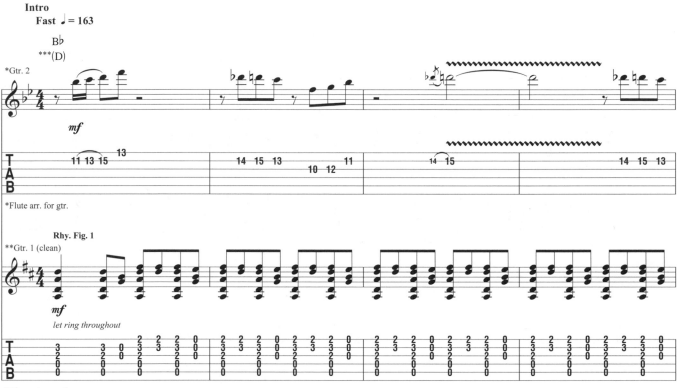

*Gtr. 2

*Flute arr. for gtr.

Rhy. Fig. 1
**Gtr. 1 (clean)

let ring throughout

**Two gtrs. arr. for one.
***Symbols in parentheses represent chord names respective to capoed guitar.
Symbols above reflect actual sounding chords. Capoed fret is "0" in tab.

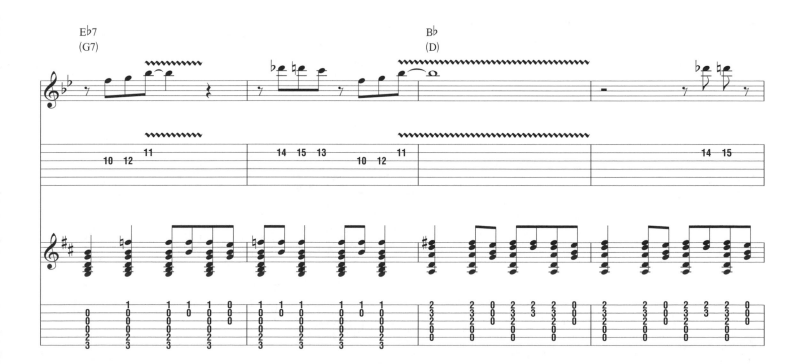

To Coda 2 ⊕

Verse

Gtr. 1: w/ Rhy. Fig. 1

- in' up the coun - try. Ba - by, don't you wan - na go? ____
- in', I'm go - ing where the wa - ter tastes ___ like wine.
___ this cit - y, got to get ___ a - way. ___
pack your leav - ing trunk, you know we've got to leave to - day. Just ex - act - ly where we

I'm go - in' up the coun - try. Ba - by, don't you wan - na go?
I'm go - ing where the wa - ter tastes ___ like
I'm gon-na leave ___ this cit - y, got to get ___ a - way.
go - in', I can - not say but we might e - ven leave the U. S. A. ___

___ wine. I'm go - in' to some place ___ where I've
___ We can jump in the wa - ter,
___ All this fuss - ing and fight - ing, man, ___ you know ___
___ 'Cause there's a brand ___ new game ___ that I ___

【 1., 3. 】

nev - er been ___ be - fore. ___
stay drunk all the time.
___ I sure can't stay.
___ want to play. ___

2. I'm go -
4. Now, ba - by,

86

from Doyle Bramhall II & Smokestack - *Welcome*

Green Light Girl

Written by Doyle Bramhall II and Susannah Melvoin

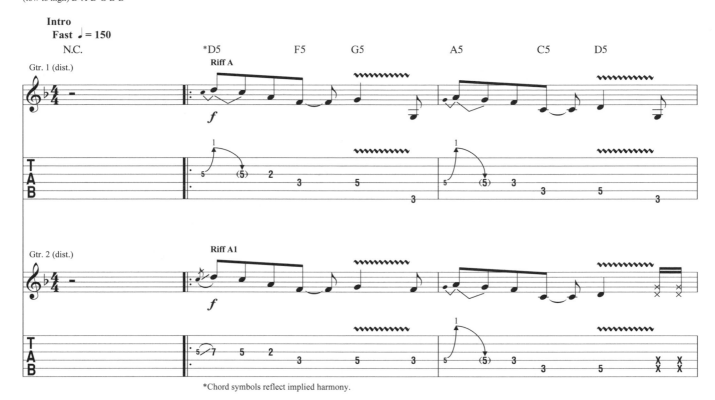

*Chord symbols reflect implied harmony.

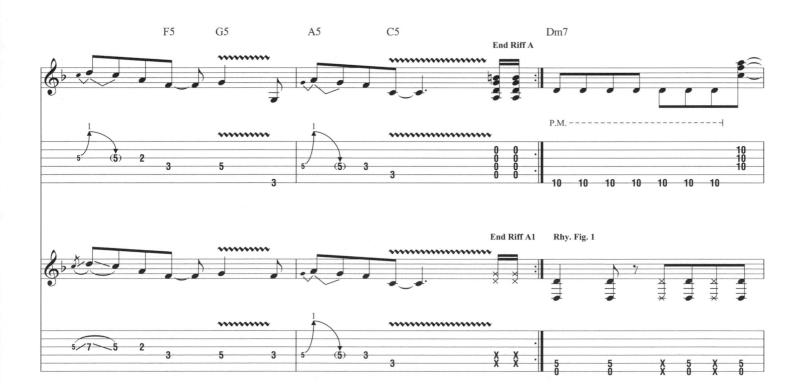

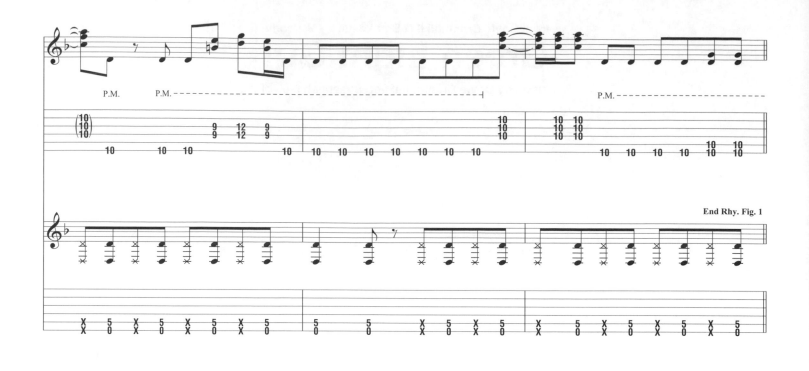

End Rhy. Fig. 1

Verse

Gtr. 2: w/ Rhy. Fig. 1 (2 times)

Dm7

1. Pret - ty thing ___ on her feet.   She's gon - na leave 'em sor - ry.
2. All the boys want you,   your glam - or and de - spair.   She

Gtr. 1

P.M.

She's a sweet 'n' so - ur miss.   Too hot to han - dle now. ___
smiles ___ and rolls her eyes ___   in a rock 'n' roll up - rise. ___

P.M.

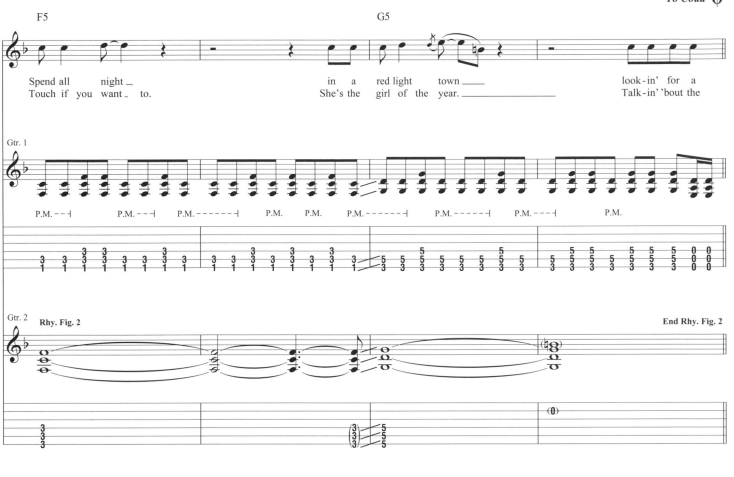

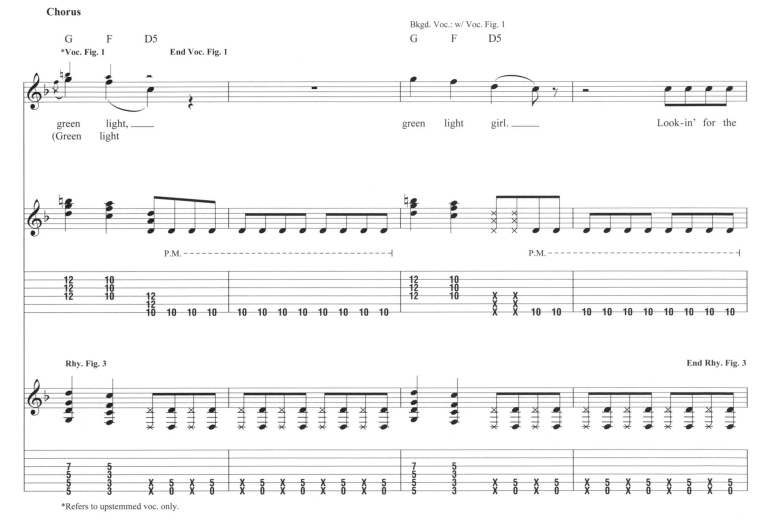

*Refers to upstemmed voc. only.

Interlude

D.S. al Coda

⊕ Coda

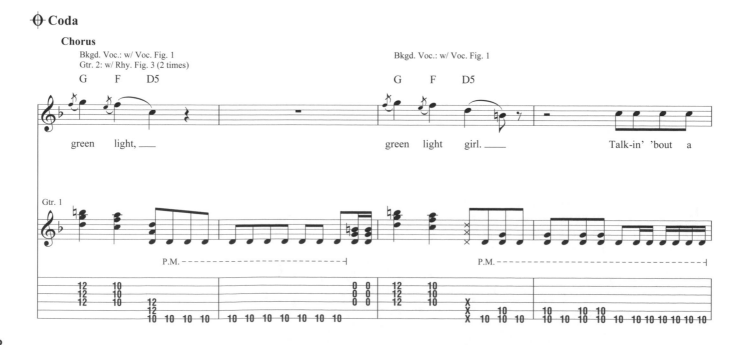

green light, _____ yeah, ba - by, green light _ girl. _____

Interlude

Gtr. 2: w/ Riff A1 (2 times)

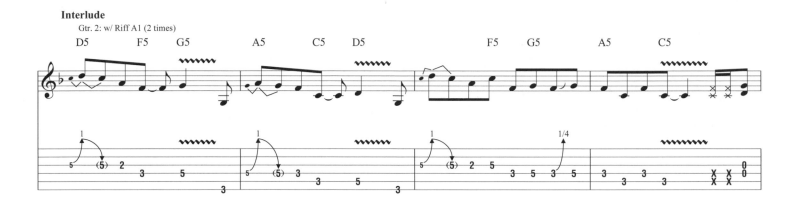

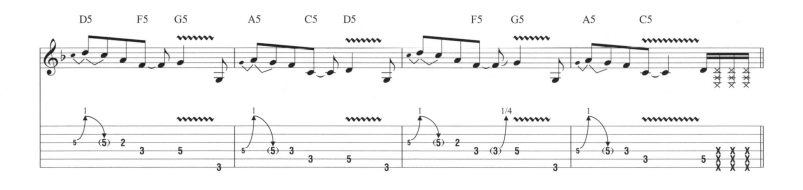

Guitar Solo

Gtr. 2: w/ Rhy. Fig. 1 (2 times)

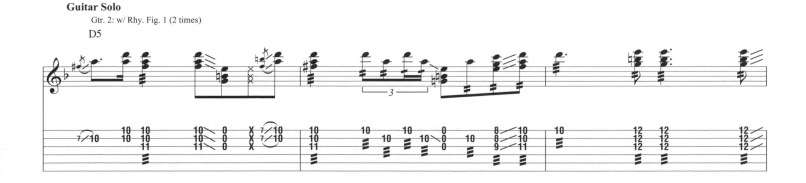

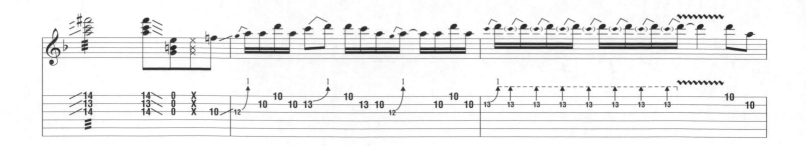

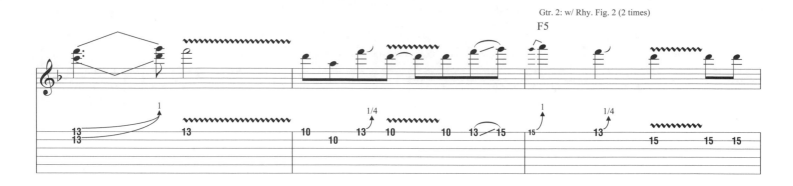

Gtr. 2: w/ Rhy. Fig. 2 (2 times)

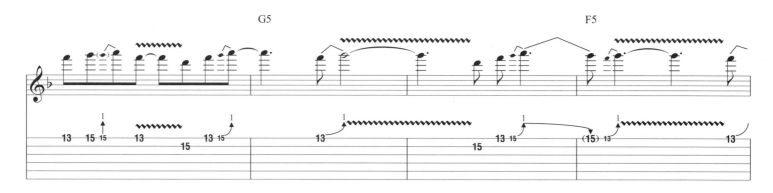

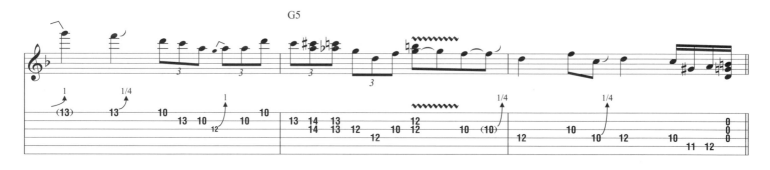

Chorus

Bkgd. Voc.: w/ Voc. Fig. 1
Gtr. 2: w/ Rhy. Fig. 3 (4 times)

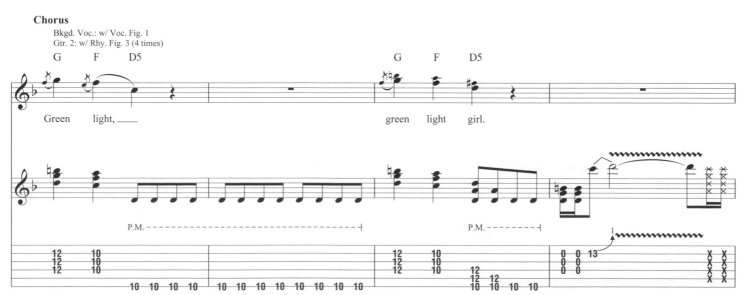

Green   light, ___   green   light   girl.

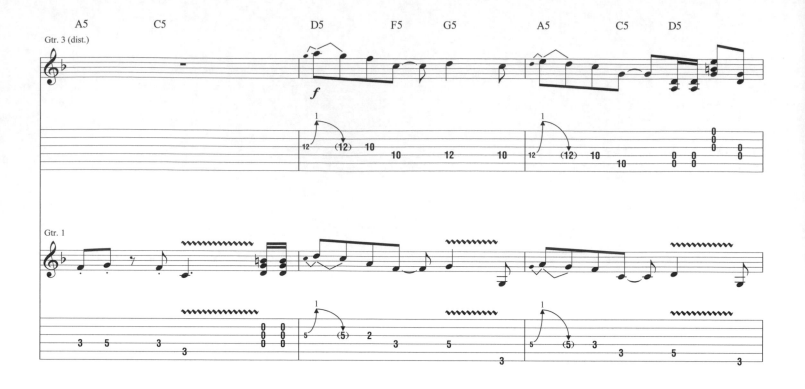

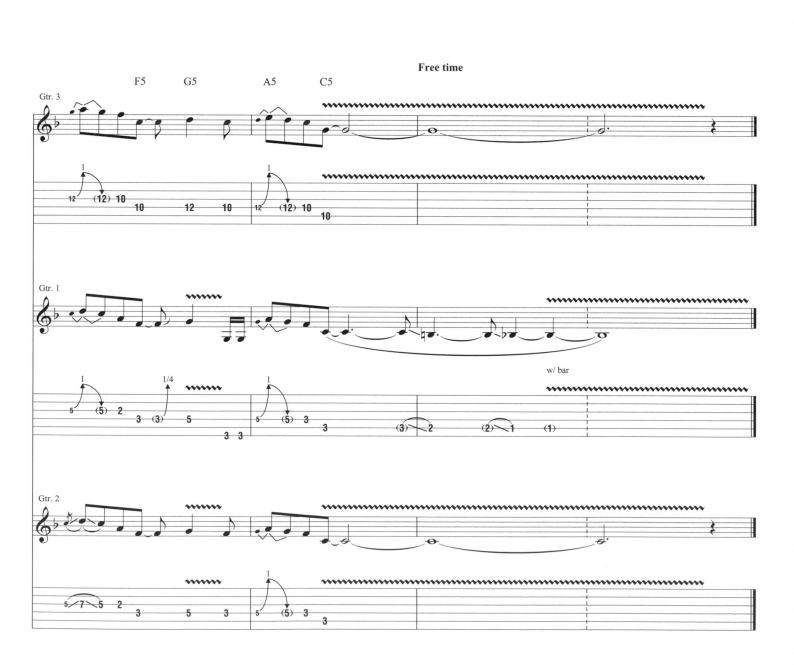

from Fleetwood Mac - *Men of the World: The Early Years*

The Green Manalishi

Words and Music by Peter Green

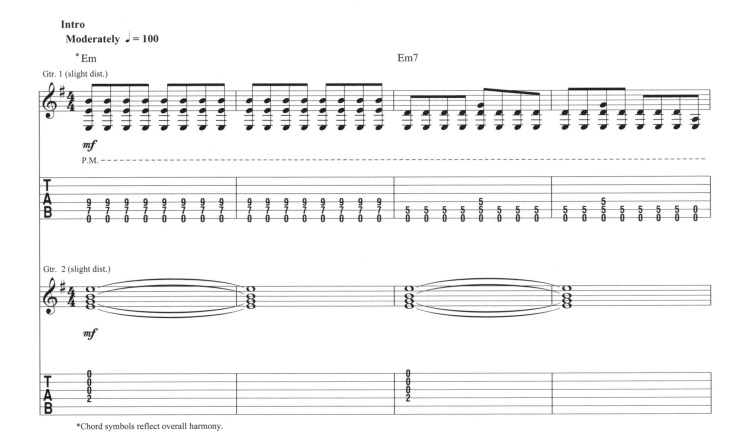

*Chord symbols reflect overall harmony.

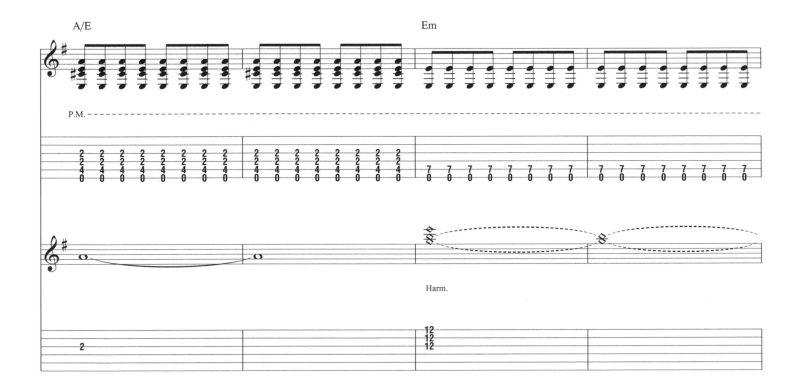

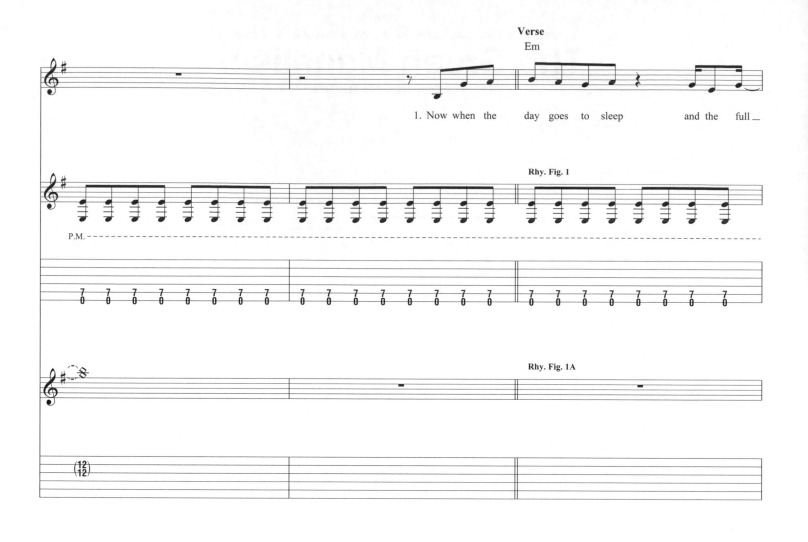

Gtrs. 1 & 2: w/ Rhy. Figs. 1 & 1A

night is ___ so black ___ that the ___ dark - ness cooks. ___   Then you come ___

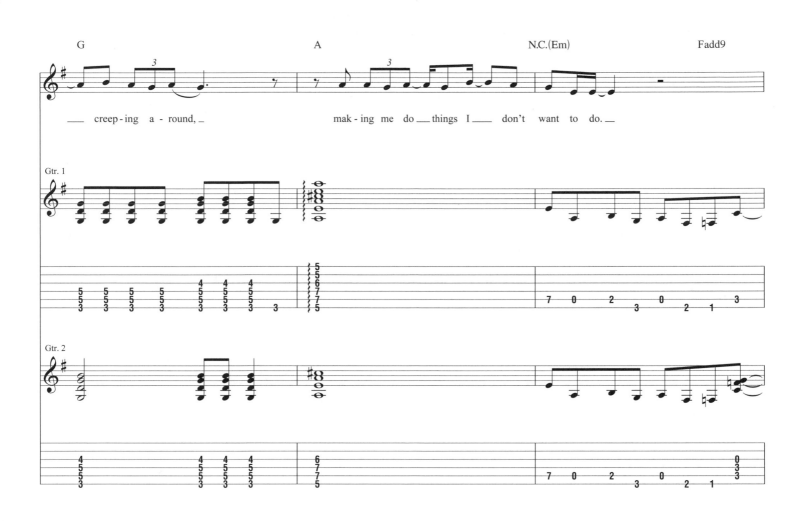

___ creep - ing a - round, ___   mak - ing me do ___ things I ___ don't want to do. ___

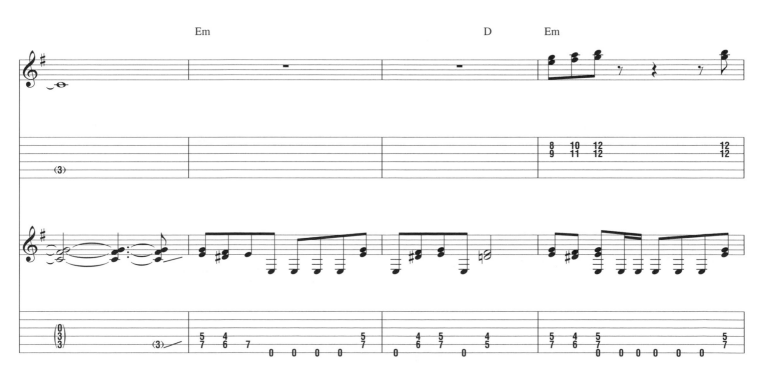

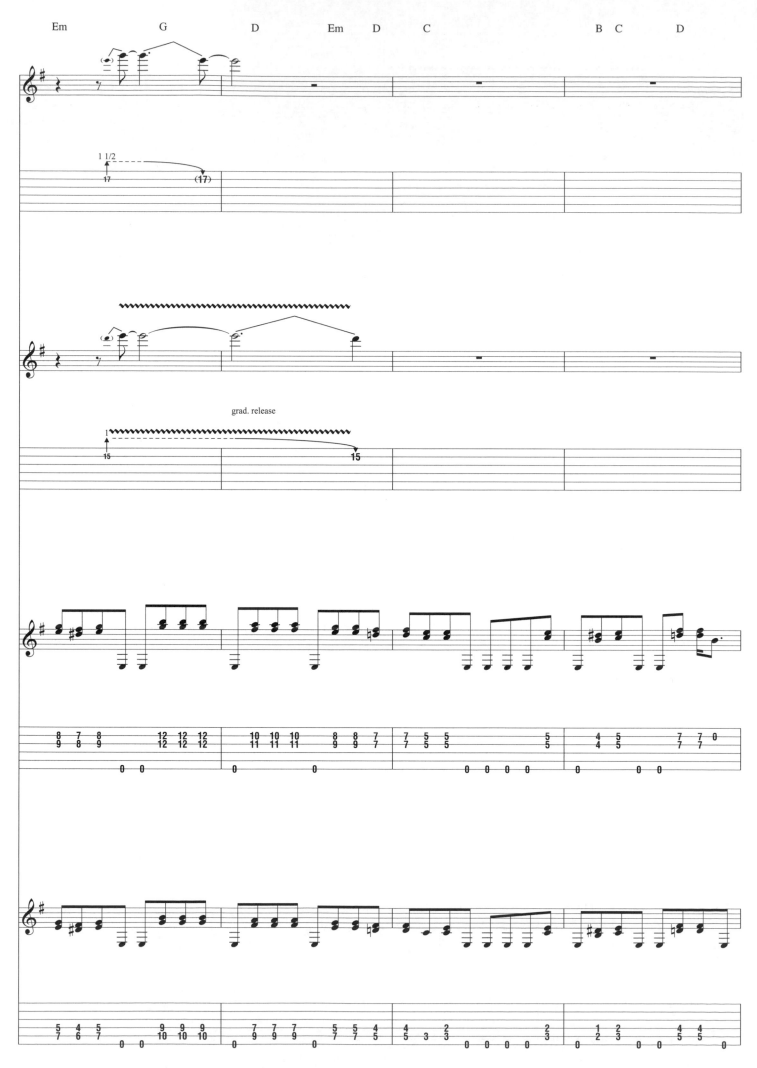

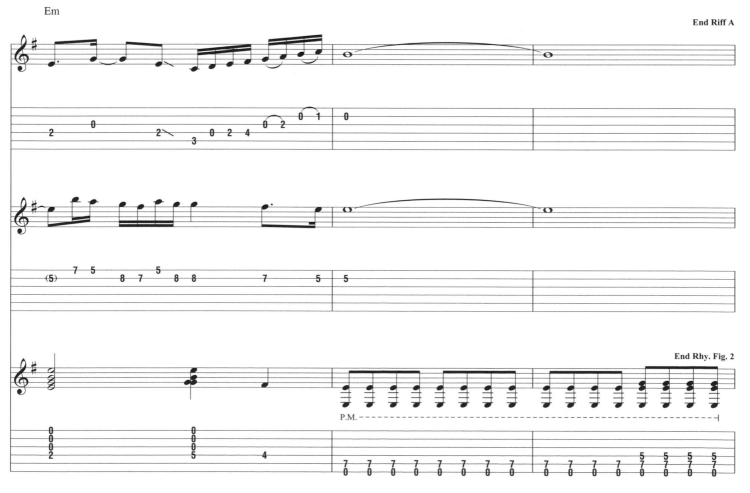

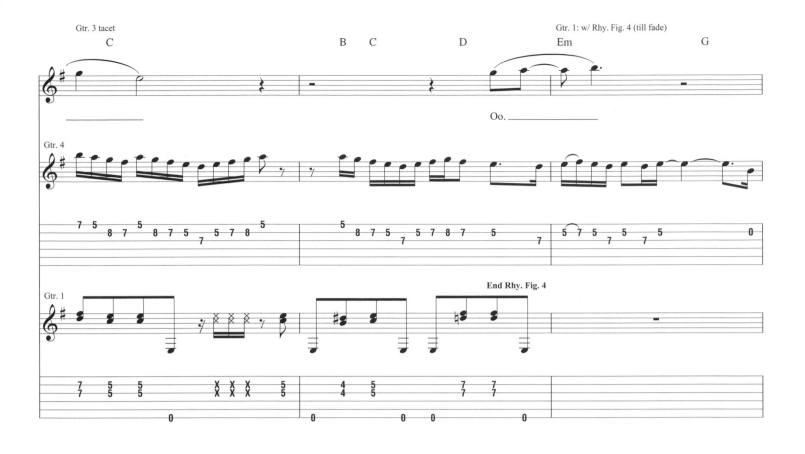

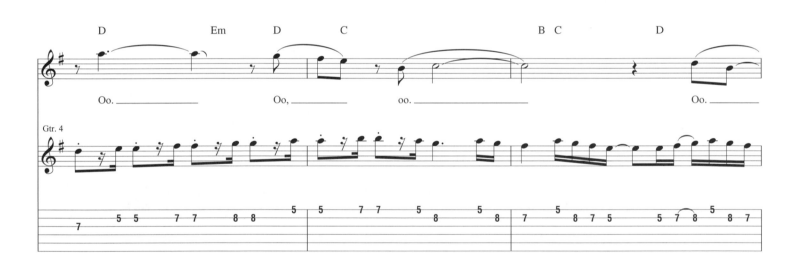

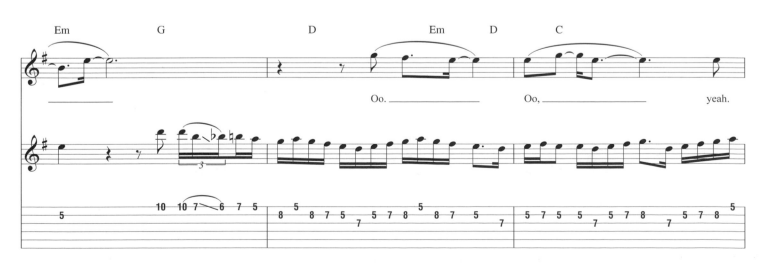

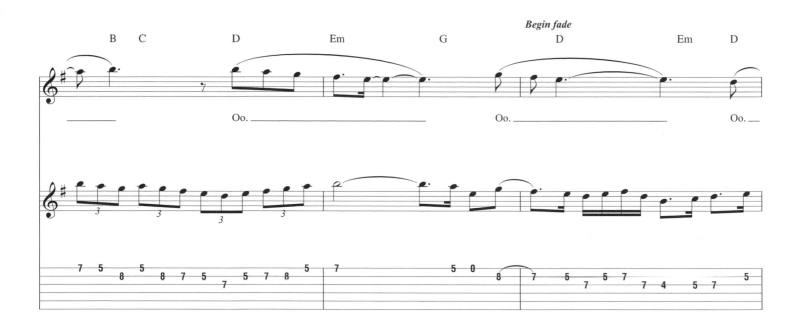

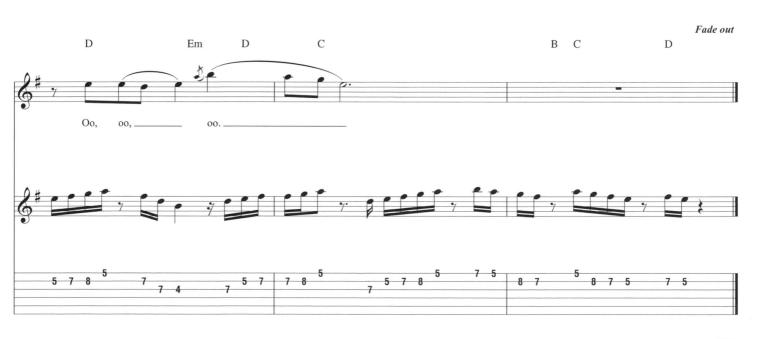

The Hunter

Words and Music by Stephen Cropper, Booker T. Jones, Al Jackson, Jr., Donald Dunn and Carl Wells

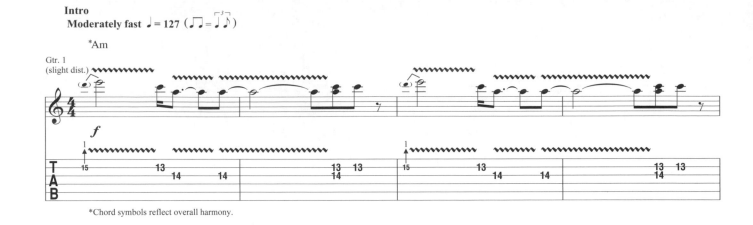

*Chord symbols reflect overall harmony.

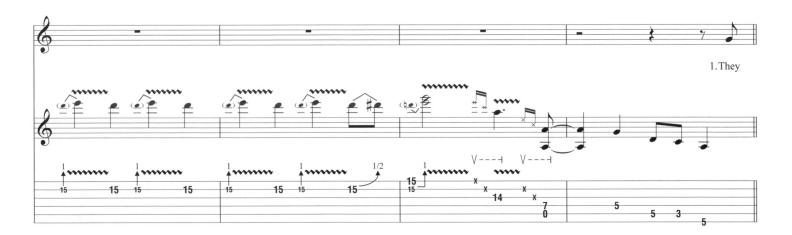

pret - ty lit - tle wom-an like you ____ is my on - ly game. ____ I

bought me a love ____ gun just the ____ oth - er day, _____

and I aim ____ to aim it your way. ____

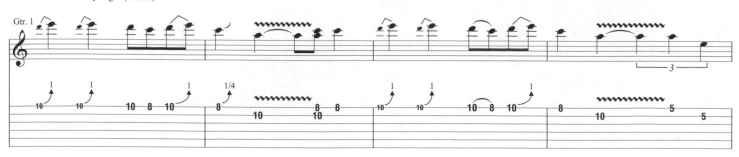

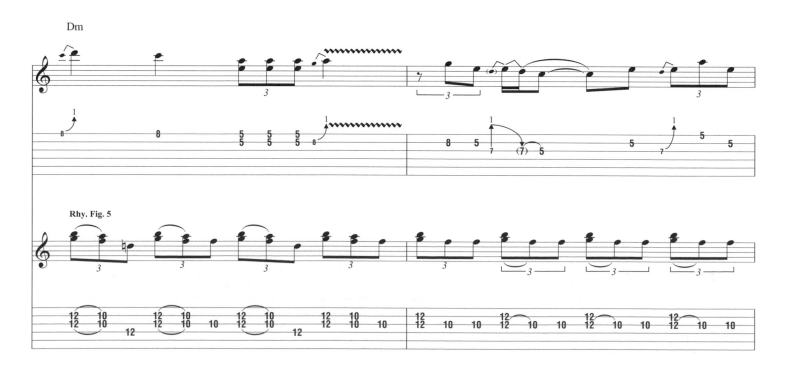

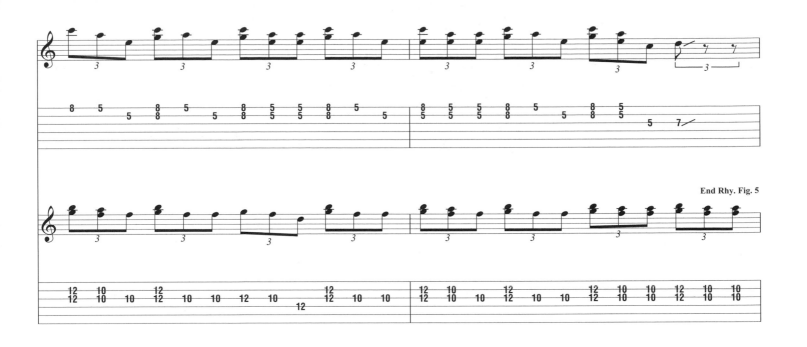

End Rhy. Fig. 5

Gtr. 2: w/ Rhy. Fig. 4 (2 times)

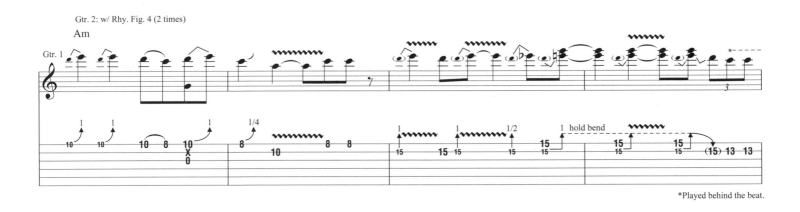

*Played behind the beat.

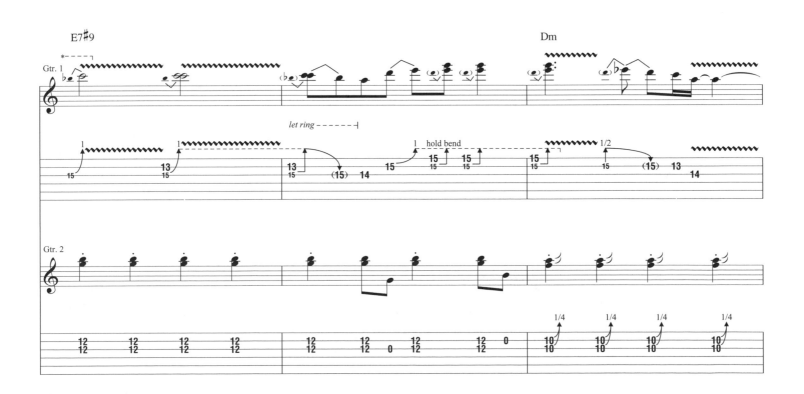

Am

E7#9

Gtr. 2: w/ Rhy. Fig. 4 (2 1/2 times)

A

Riff D

End Riff D

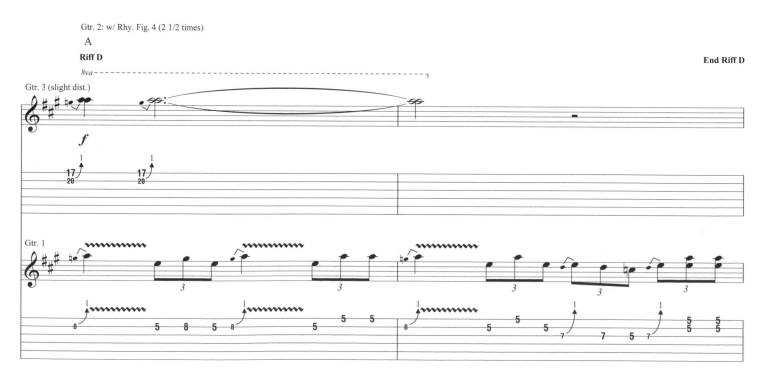

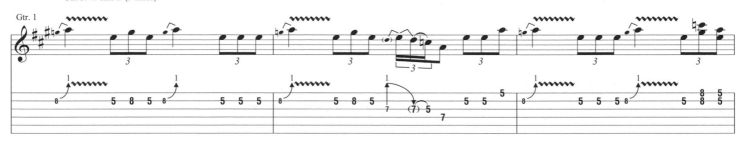

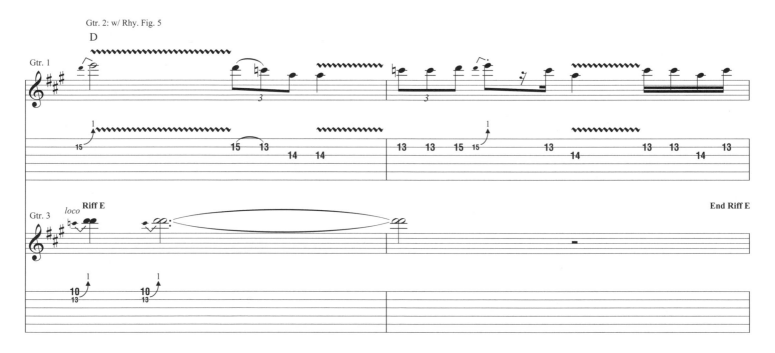

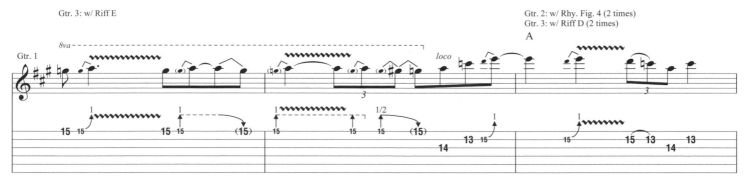

Hey,

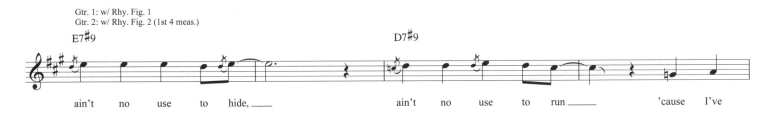

Gtr. 1: w/ Rhy. Fig. 1
Gtr. 2: w/ Rhy. Fig. 2 (1st 4 meas.)

E7#9   D7#9

ain't   no   use   to   hide,____   ain't   no   use   to   run____   'cause I've

A   E7#9

got   you   in   the   sight____   of   my   girl - y   gun.   3. The

Gtr. 2

Gtr. 1

P.M.

Verse

Gtr. 1: w/ Riff A (2 times)
Gtr. 2: w/ Riff B

A

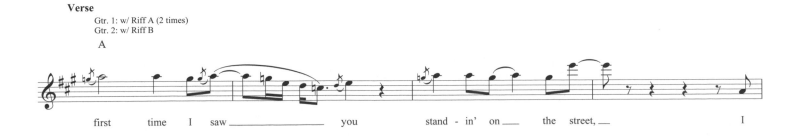

first   time   I   saw_____   you   stand - in'   on____   the   street,____   I

said to my-self, _____ "Oo! Ain't she sweet?" ___ I

got my love__ gun__ load - ed ___ with hun-dreds of kiss - es. _____ As

soon as I pull the trig - ger, ba - by, there will be ___ no

miss - es. Ain't no use to hide, _____

ain't no use to run _____ 'cause I've got you in the sight ___

Gtr. 1: w/ Rhy. Fig. 3

E7#9

of my girl - y gun.

P.M.

Outro

A

Gtr. 1

Gtr. 2

E7#9

120

Just Got Paid

Words and Music by Billy F Gibbons and Bill Ham

*Chord symbols reflect implied harmony.

**Slide positioned halfway between the 11th & 12th frets.

Verse

*E   D   Em7

1. Just got paid to-day, ___ got me a pock-et full ___ of change. ___

*Chord symbols reflect overall harmony.

E   D

Said I just got paid to-day, _____ got me a pock-et full _____

Riff C

Guitar Solo

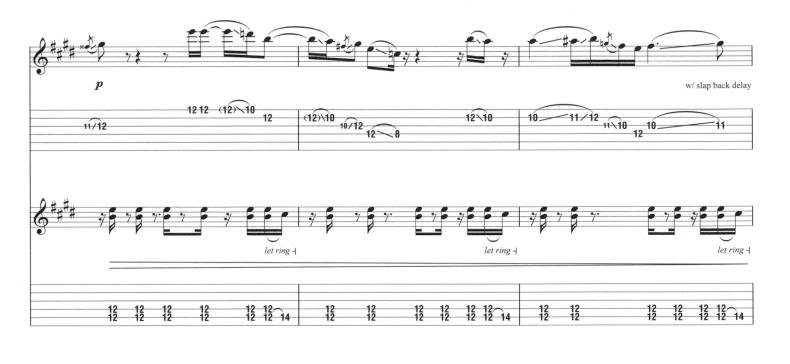

w/ slap back delay

delay off

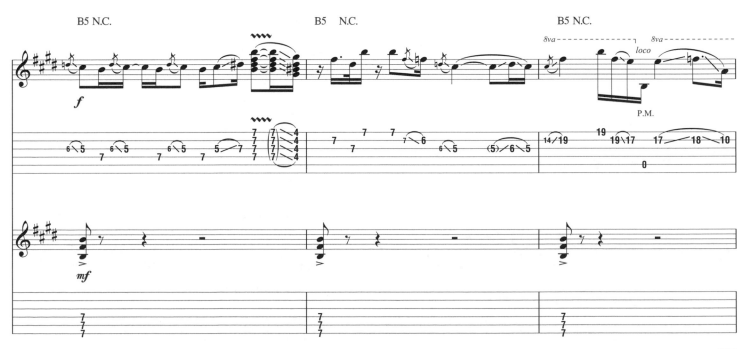

from Joe Bonamassa - *Blues Deluxe*

Left Overs

By Albert Collins

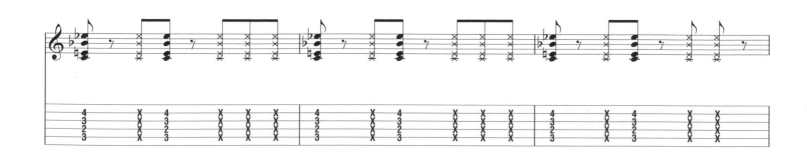

*Chord symbols reflect overall harmony.

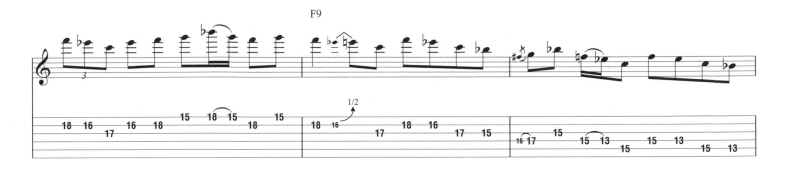

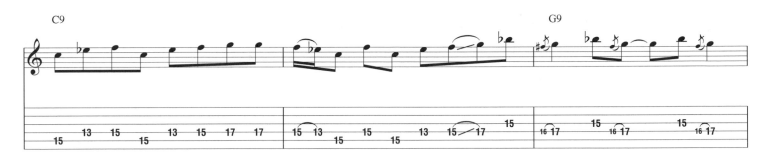

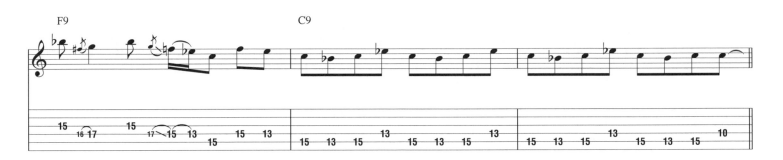

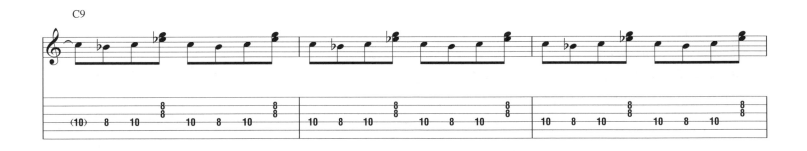

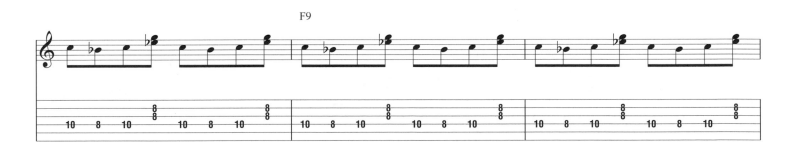

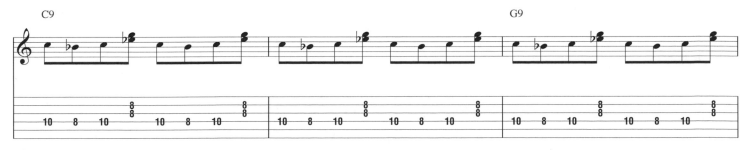

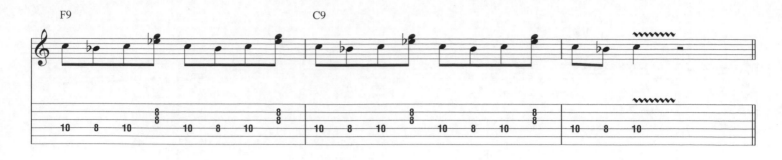

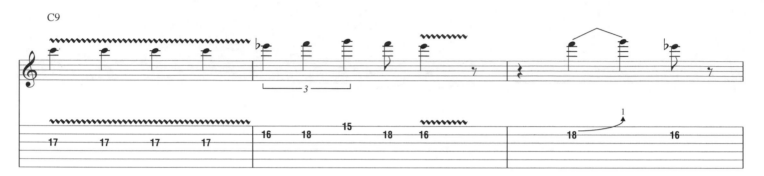

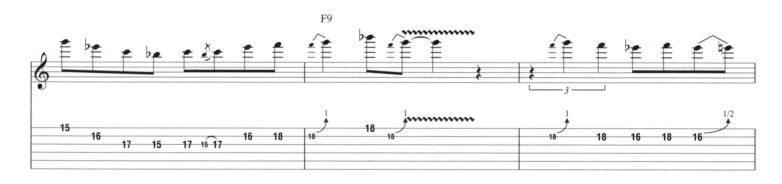

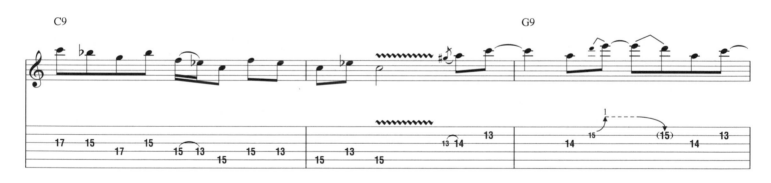

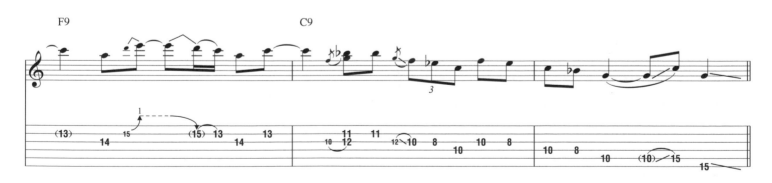

Keyboard Solo

Gtr. 1: w/ Rhy. Fig. 1

C7#9

D.C. al Coda
(with repeat)

Coda

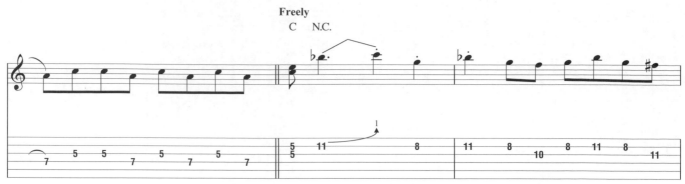

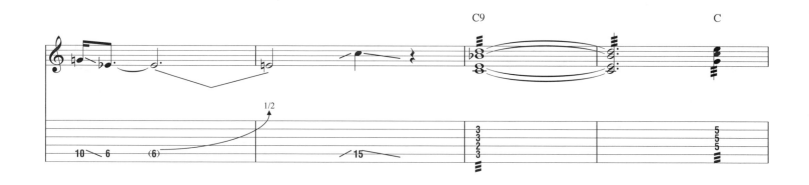

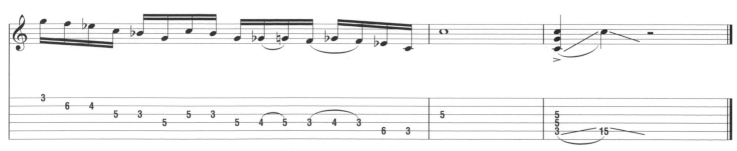

from Jonny Lang - *Lie to Me*

Lie to Me

Words and Music by David Rivkin and Bruce McCabe

Tune down 1/2 step:
(low to high) Eb-Ab-Db-Gb-Bb-Eb

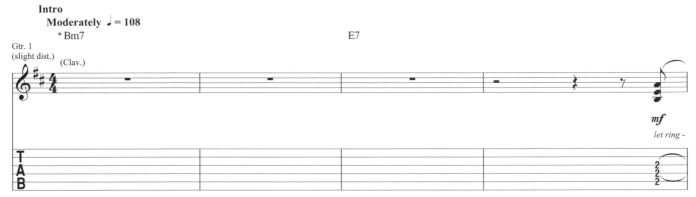

*Chord symbols reflect overall harmony.

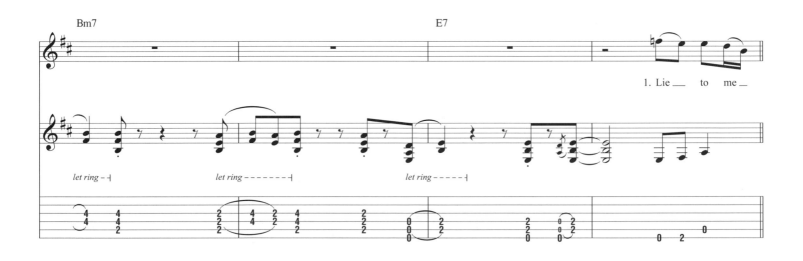

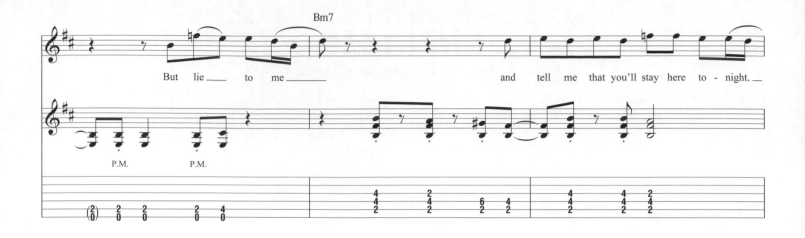

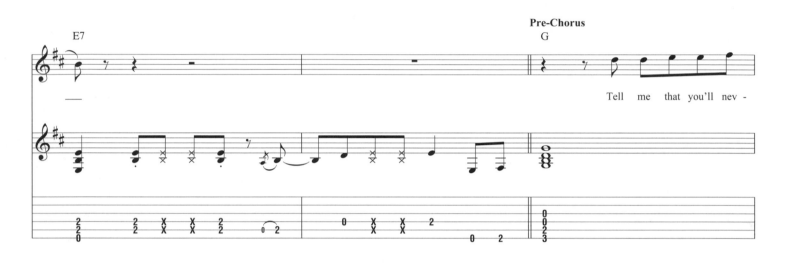

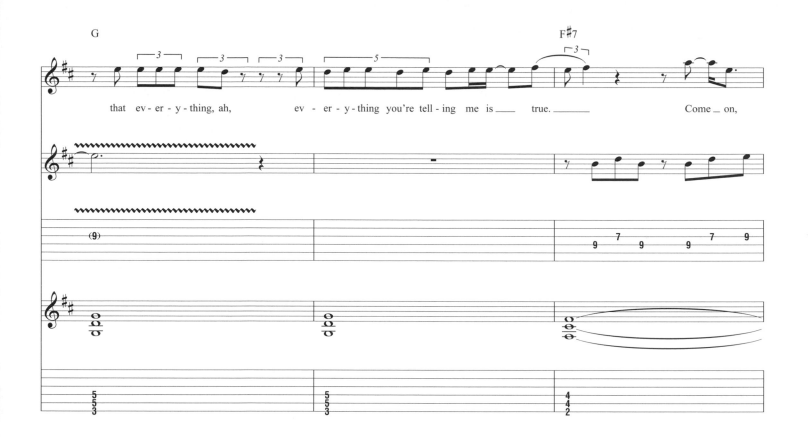

that ev-er-y-thing, ah, ev-er-y-thing you're tell-ing me is true. Come on,

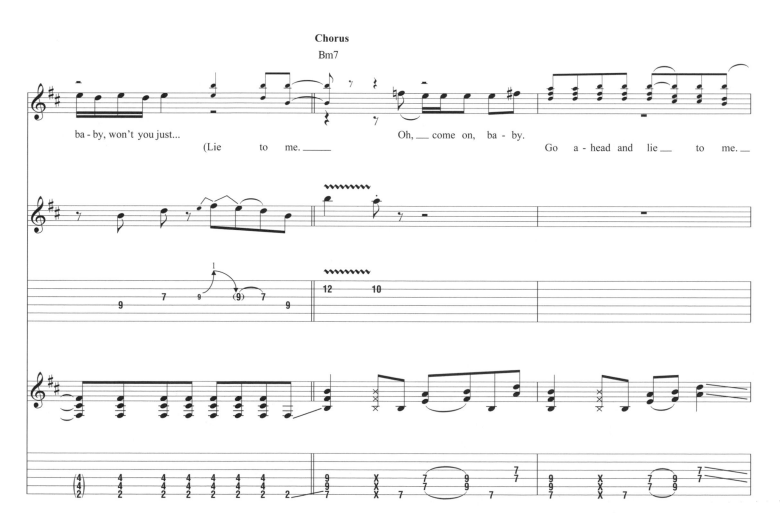

Chorus

ba-by, won't you just... Oh, come on, ba-by. Go a-head and lie to me.
(Lie to me.

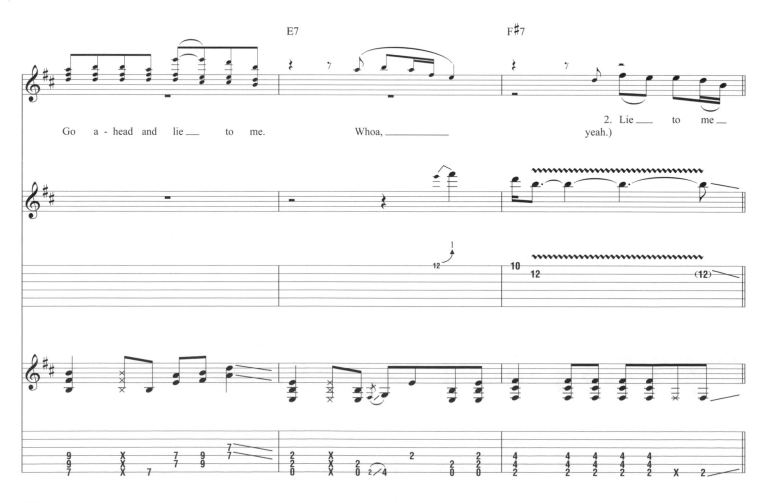

Verse

and it don't __ mat-ter an-y-more _____

and it could nev - er be _____   the way it was   be - fore. __

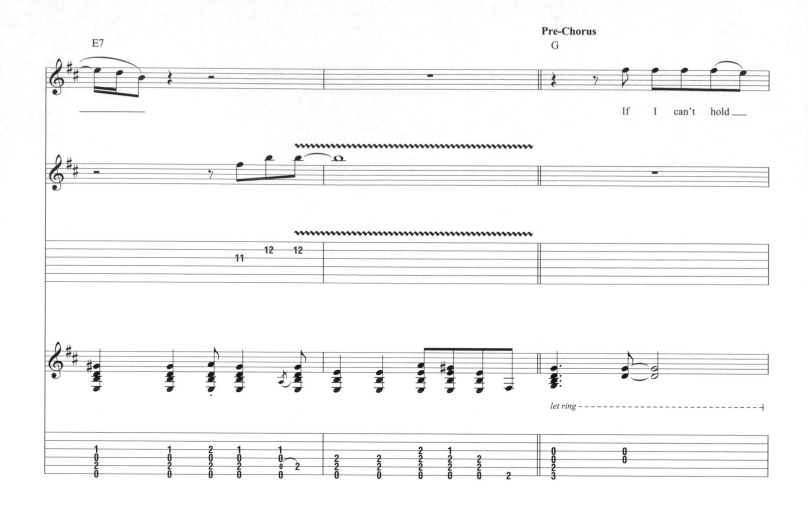

G   F#7

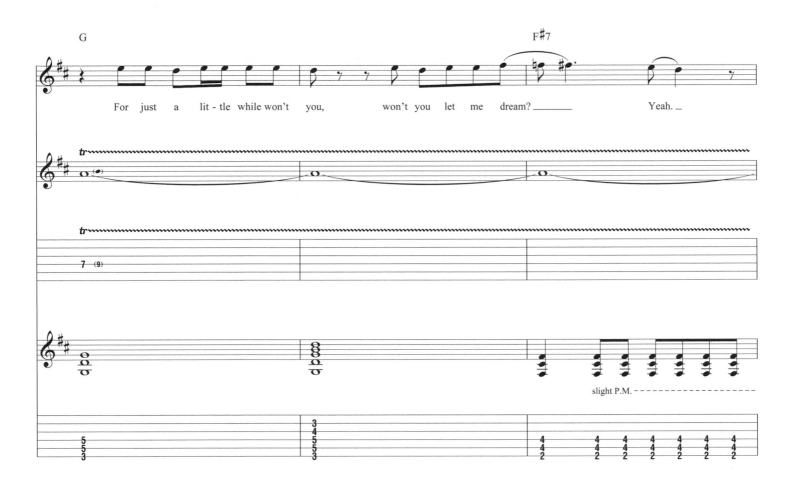

For just a lit-tle while won't you, won't you let me dream? _____ Yeah. _

Guitar Solo
Bm7

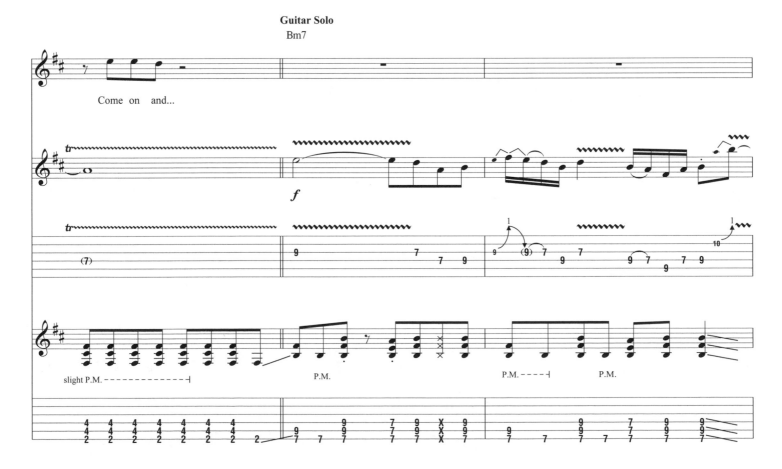

Come on and...

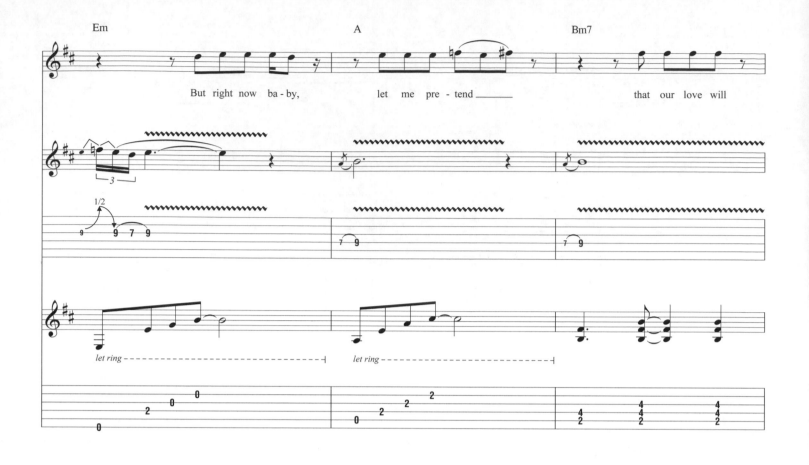

But right now ba - by,   let me pre - tend _____   that our love will

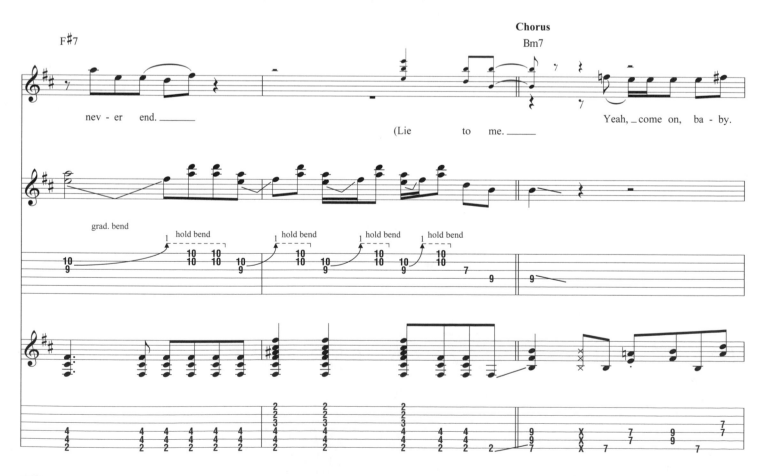

nev - er end. _____

(Lie   to   me. _____

Yeah, _come on, ba - by.

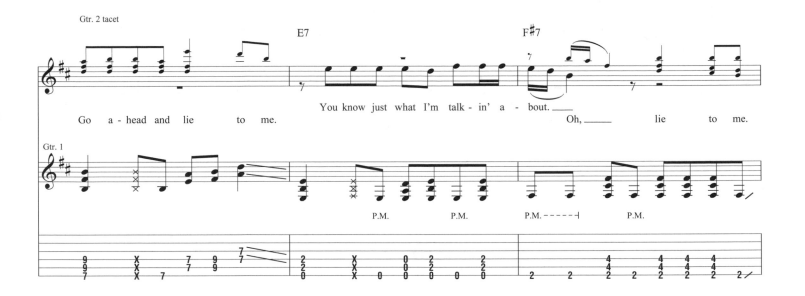

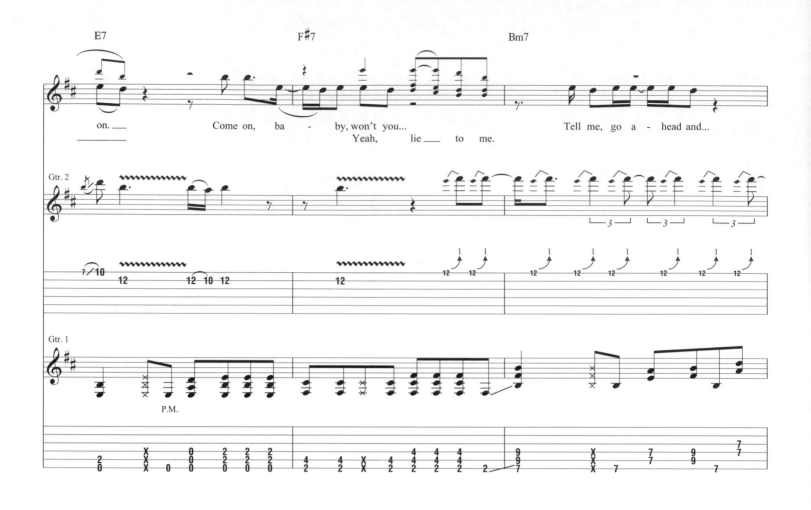

on. ___   Come on, ba - by, won't you...   Tell me, go a - head and...
___   Yeah, lie ___ to me.

Go a - head and lie ___ to me.)   Come on,   I just want you to lie ___

Outro-Guitar Solo

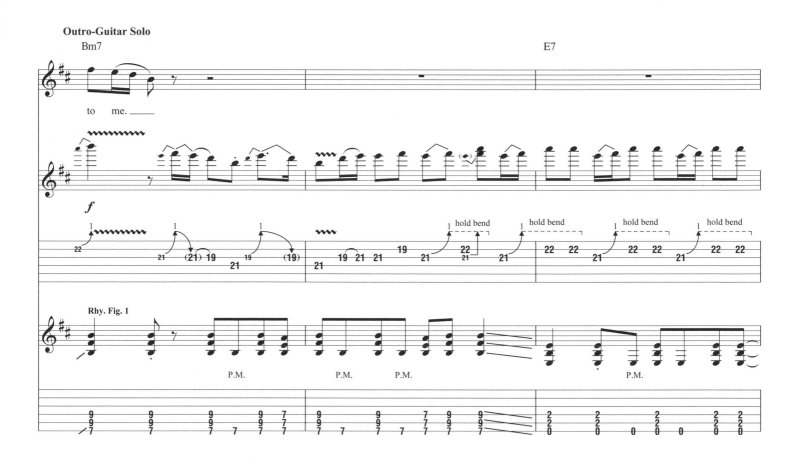

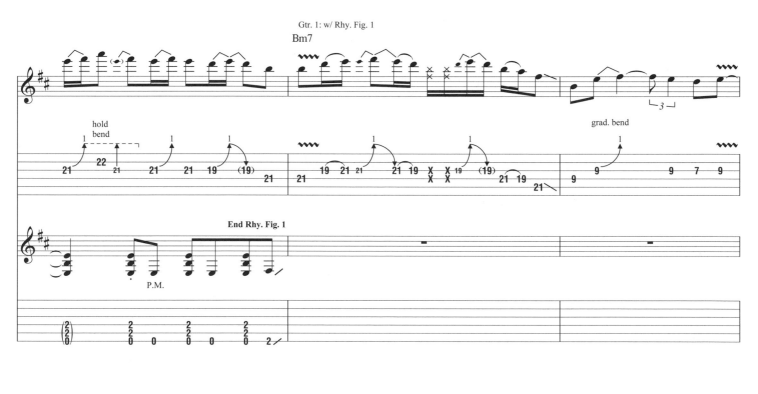

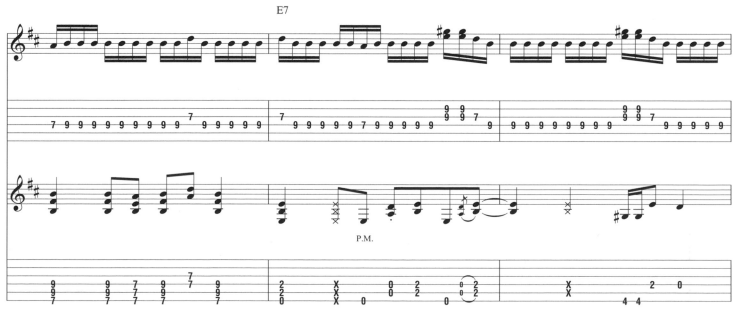

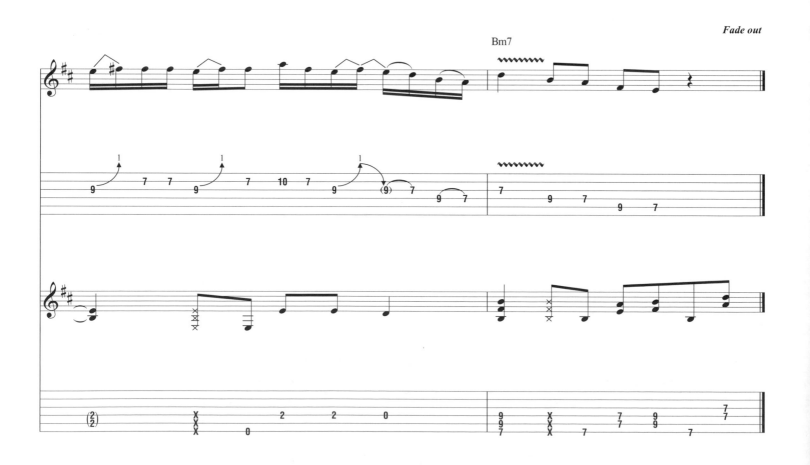

from Arc Angels - *Arc Angels*

Living in a Dream

Words and Music by Doyle Bramhall and Charles Sexton

Doyle Bramhall II: 1. If

Verse

you were _ mine, _____   I'd

give   you all __ the   world. _____   *Charlie Sexton:* If

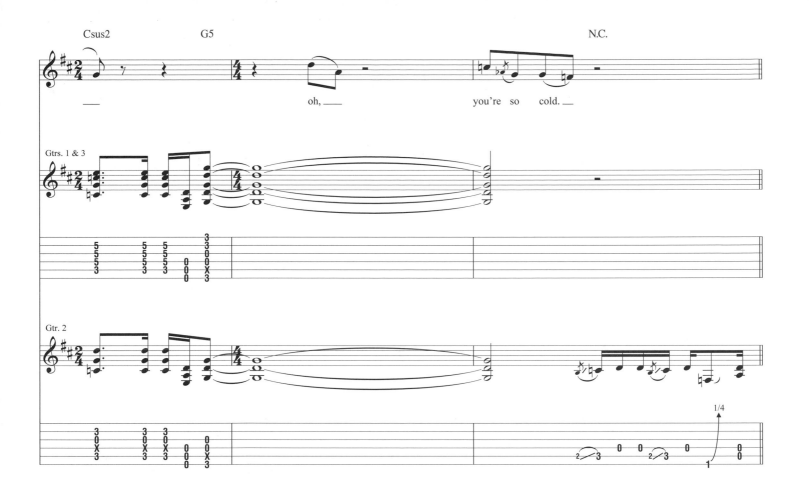

oh, ___ you're so cold. ___

Interlude

Gtr. 1: w/ Rhy. Fig. 1
Gtr. 3: w/ Riff A

Gtr. 3: w/ Riff C

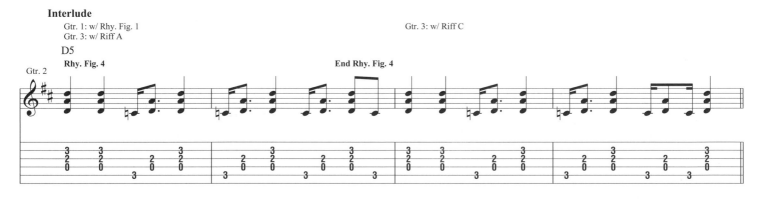

Verse

Gtrs. 1 & 2: w/ Rhy. Fig. 2
Gtr. 3: w/ Riff D (2 times)

C.S.: 2. Give me time, ___ oh, time is all ___ we ___ need.

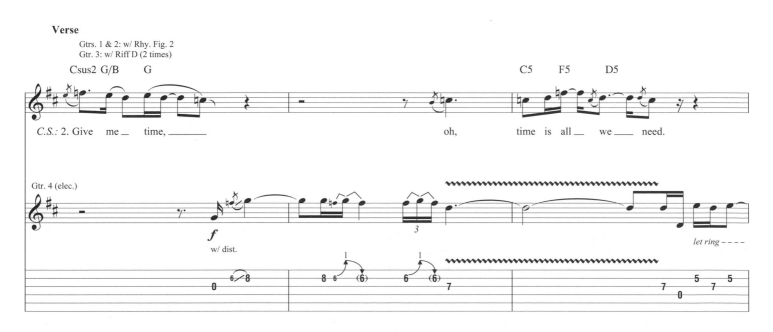

159

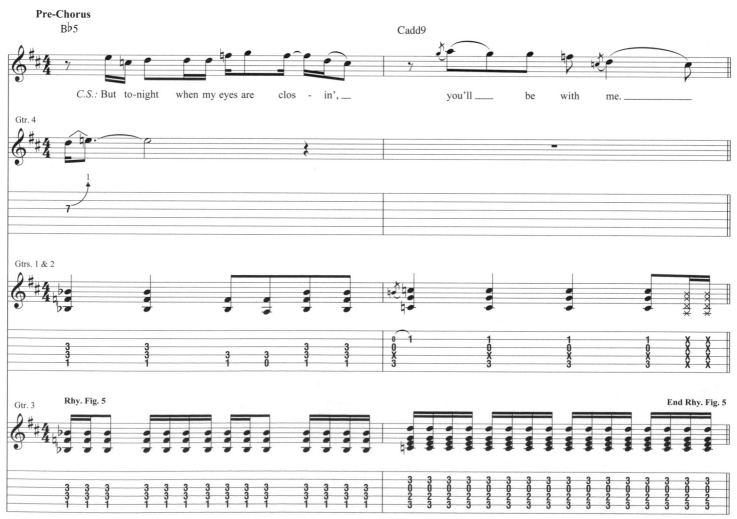

§ **Chorus**

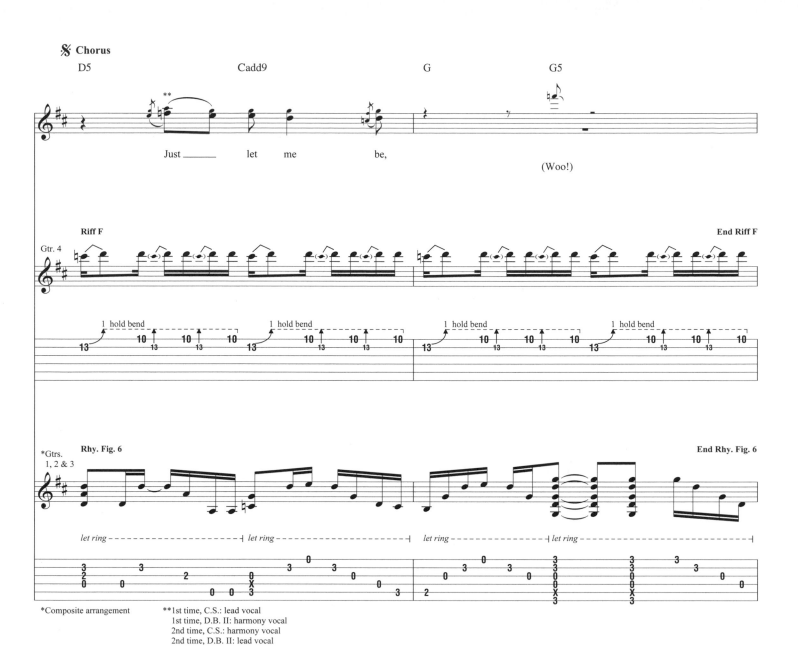

Just ____ let me be,

(Woo!)

*Composite arrangement   **1st time, C.S.: lead vocal
1st time, D.B. II: harmony vocal
2nd time, C.S.: harmony vocal
2nd time, D.B. II: lead vocal

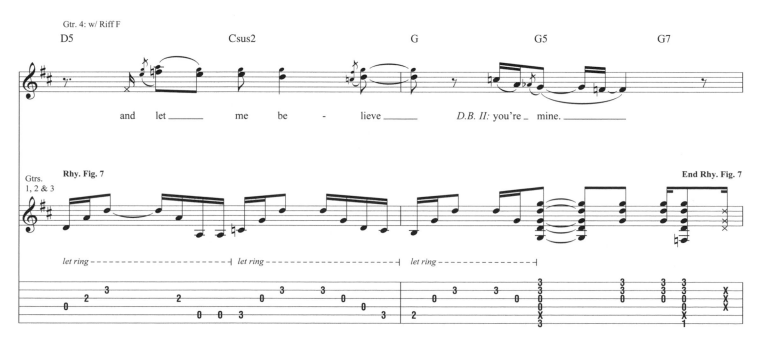

and let ____ me be - lieve ____ *D.B. II:* you're ____ mine. ____

Interlude
   Gtr. 1: w/ Rhy. Fig. 1 (1st 2 meas.)
   Gtr. 2: w/ Rhy. Fig. 4
   Gtr. 3: w/ Riff A

D5

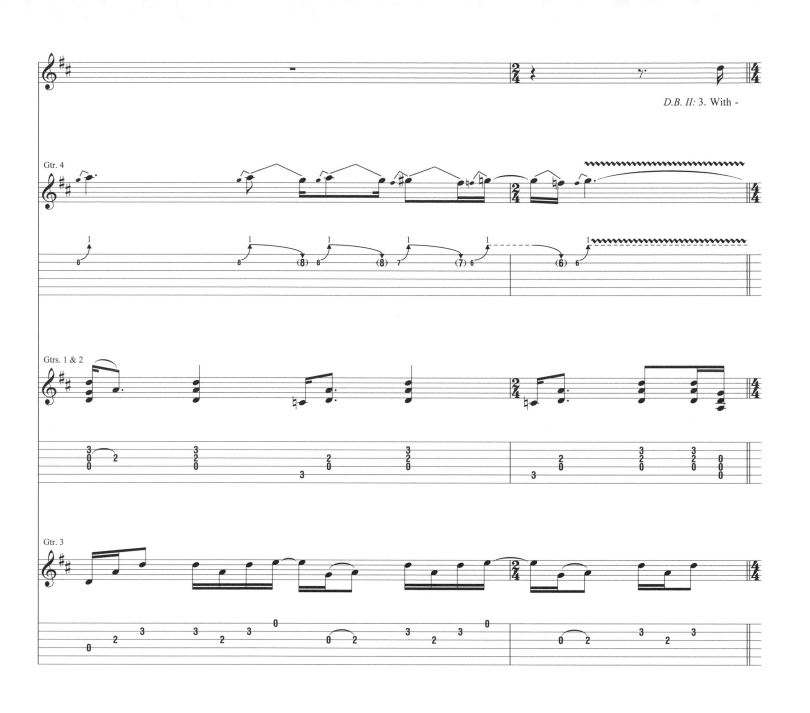

D.B. II: 3. With -

Verse

Gtrs. 1 & 2: w/ Rhy. Fig. 2
Gtr. 3: w/ Riff D (2 times)

Csus2   G/B   G   C5   F5   D5

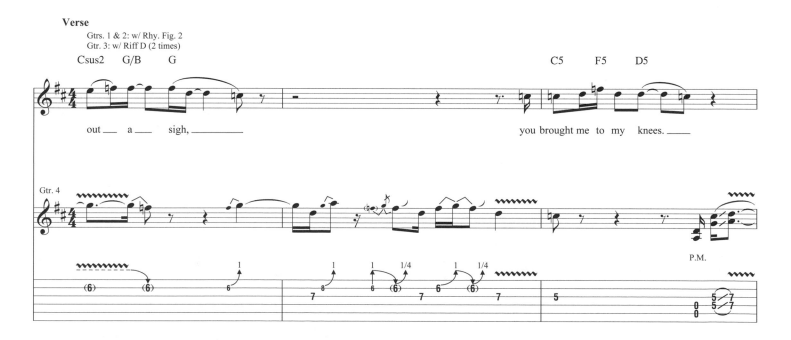

out __ a __ sigh, _____   you brought me to my knees. _____

Gtrs. 1 & 2: w/ Rhy. Fig. 3

Csus2   G/B   G

C.S.: With - out   a ___ sign, _____   I crossed the line. _   I ___

P.M.   P.M.   P.M. ─┤   P.M.   P.M.

Gtr. 3: w/ Riff E

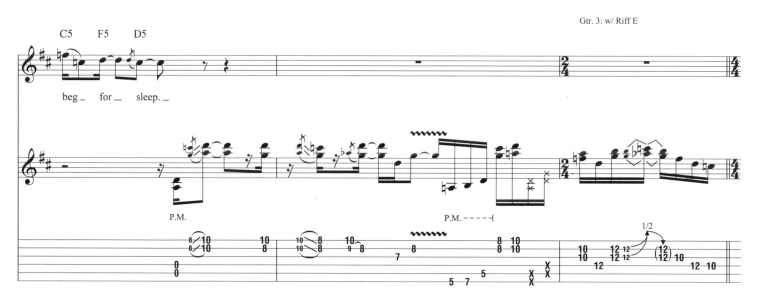

C5   F5   D5

beg _ for _ sleep. _

P.M.   P.M. ─ ─ ─ ─ ─┤

D.S. al Coda

Pre-Chorus

Gtr. 3: w/ Rhy. Fig. 5 (1st meas.)   Gtr. 4 tacet

B♭5   C5

D.B. II: But to-night   when my eyes are   clos - in', _   You will   be   with   me.

Gtr. 4

let ring - ─┤

Gtrs. 1 & 2

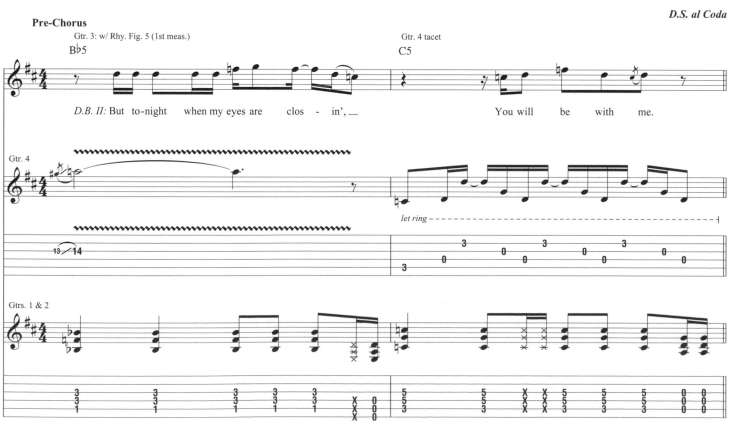

Coda

Gtr. 4 tacet

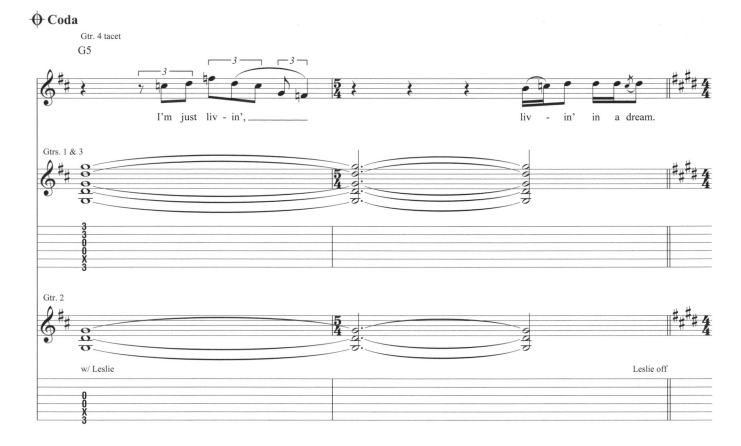

I'm just liv - in', _____ liv - in' in a dream.

Gtrs. 1 & 3

Gtr. 2

w/ Leslie

Leslie off

Guitar Solo

N.C.   E

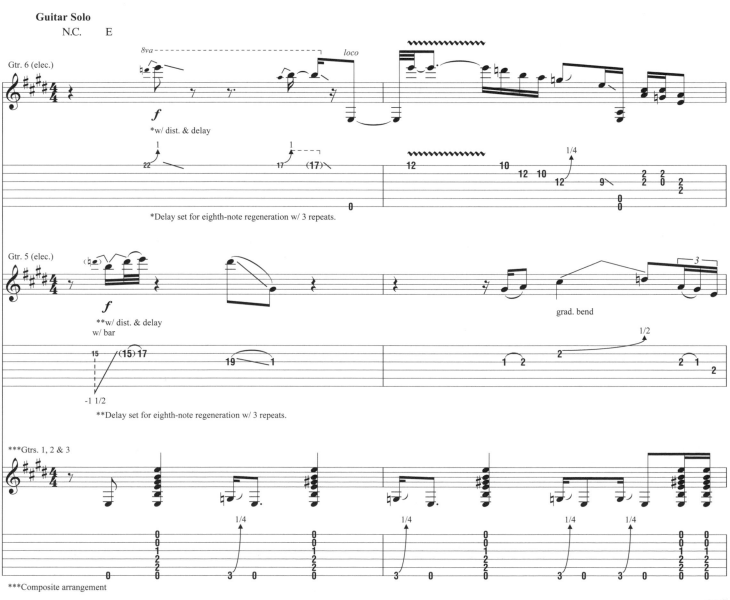

Gtr. 6 (elec.)

*w/ dist. & delay

*Delay set for eighth-note regeneration w/ 3 repeats.

Gtr. 5 (elec.)

**w/ dist. & delay
w/ bar

grad. bend

**Delay set for eighth-note regeneration w/ 3 repeats.

***Gtrs. 1, 2 & 3

***Composite arrangement

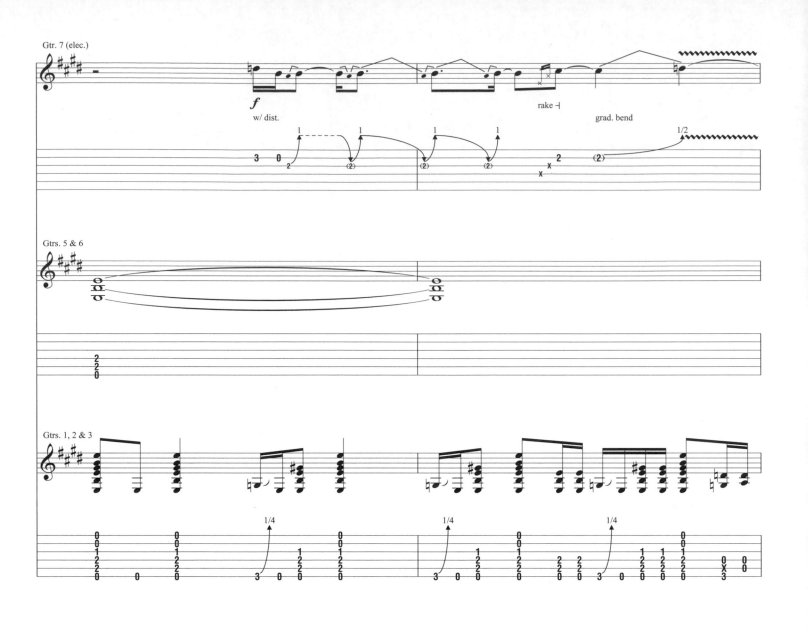

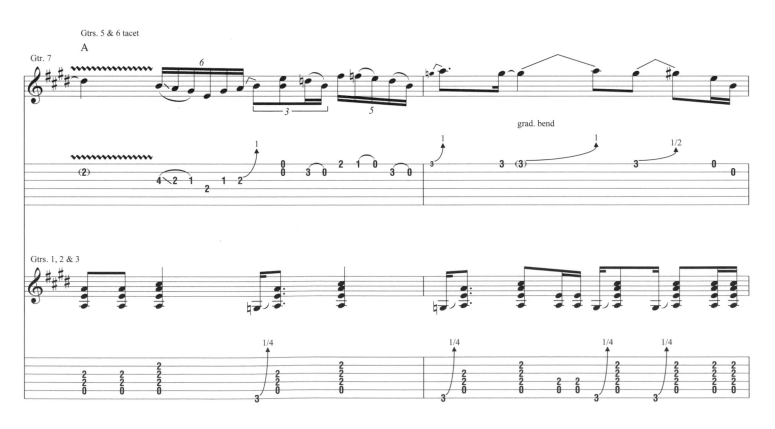

166

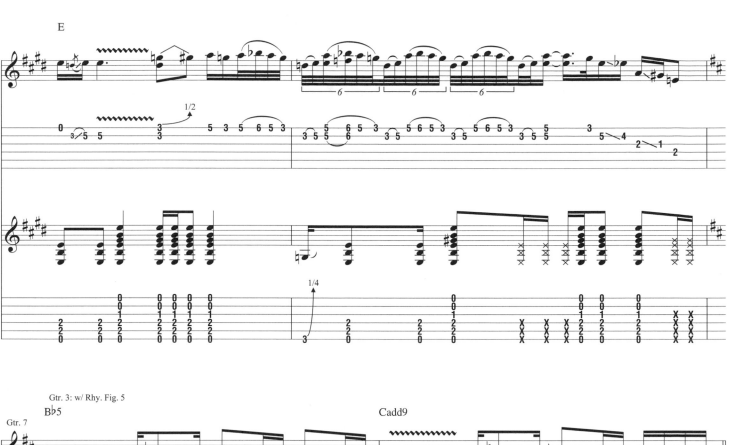

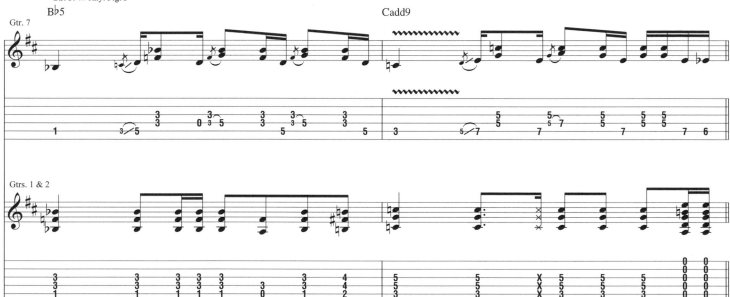

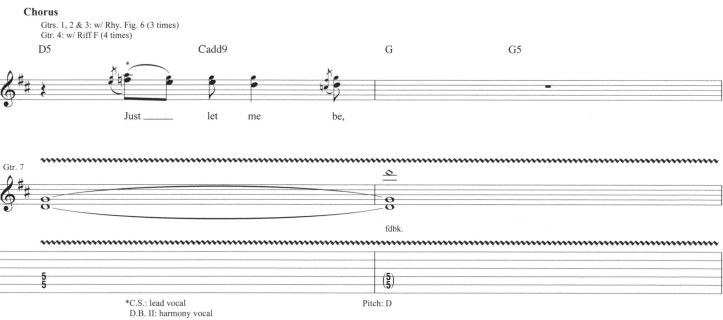

and let ___ me be - lieve ___ you're ___ mine. ___ Just ___ let me be,

Gtrs. 1, 2 & 3: w/ Rhy. Fig. 7

Let me be - lieve _____ *D.B. II:* you're mine. _____

Gtrs. 1 & 3: w/ Rhy. Fig. 8
Gtr. 2: w/ Rhy. Fig. 8A

Gtr. 4 tacet

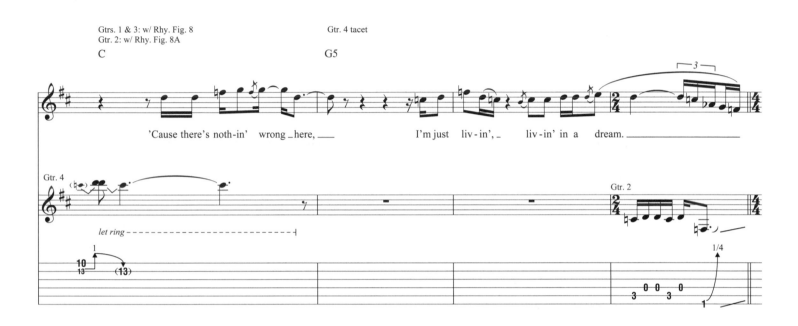

'Cause there's noth-in' wrong ___ here, ___ I'm just liv-in', ___ liv-in' in a dream. _____

Outro-Guitar Solo

Gtr. 1: w/ Rhy. Fig. 1 (1st 2 meas., 2 times)   Gtr. 2: w/ Rhy. Fig. 1 (1st 2 meas.)
Gtr. 2: w/ Rhy. Fill 1A   Gtr. 3: w/ Riff B (2 times)
Gtr. 3: w/ Riff A

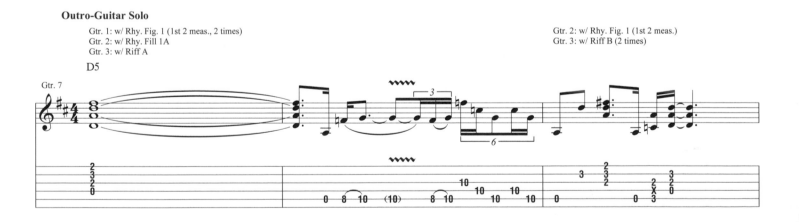

Gtrs. 1 & 2: w/ Rhy. Fills 1 & 1A

from Rory Gallagher - *Calling Card*

Moonchild

Words and Music by Rory Gallagher

Intro
Very fast ♩ = 196

N.C. (Am)

*Slight P.M. throughout

Rhy. Fig. 1   End Rhy. Fig. 1

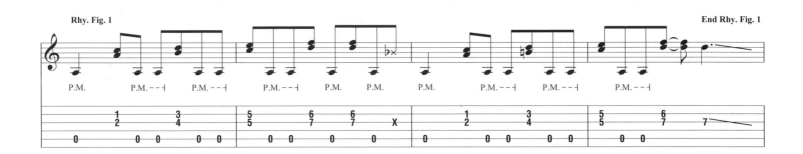

**G

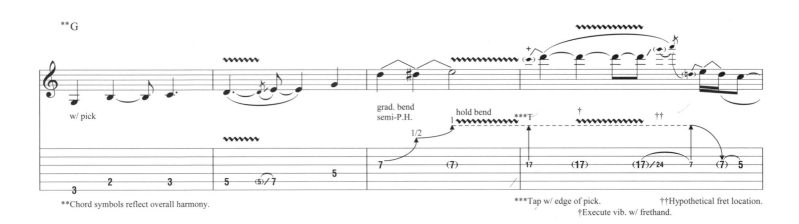

**Chord symbols reflect overall harmony.   ***Tap w/ edge of pick.   ††Hypothetical fret location.
†Execute vib. w/ frethand.

Am

*Let top three strings ring from previous meas. **T = Thumb on 6th string

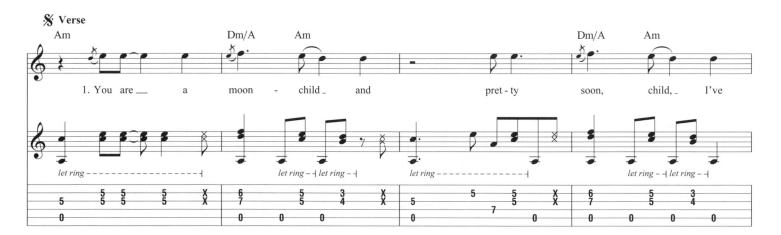

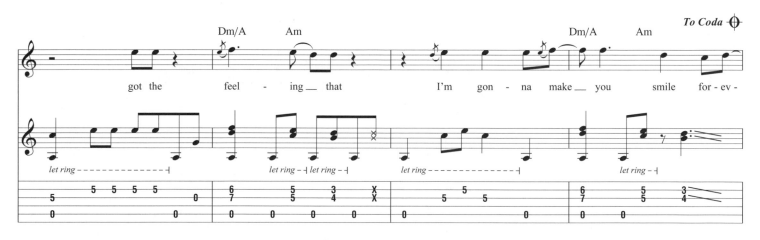

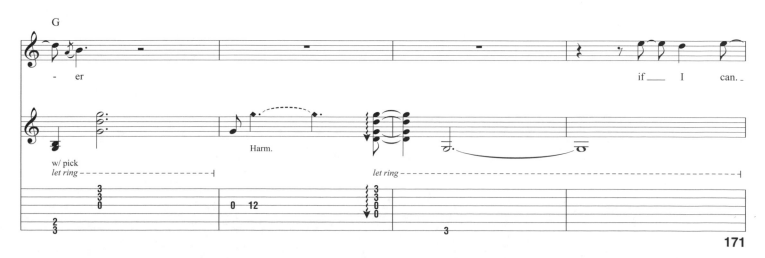

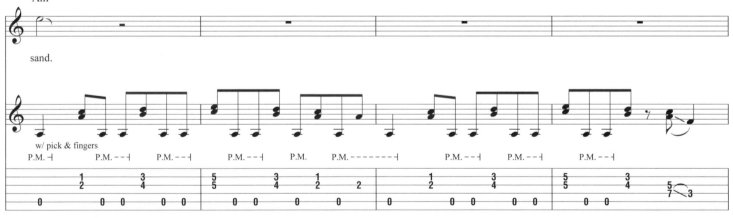

Time ____ slips   by   like   grains   of

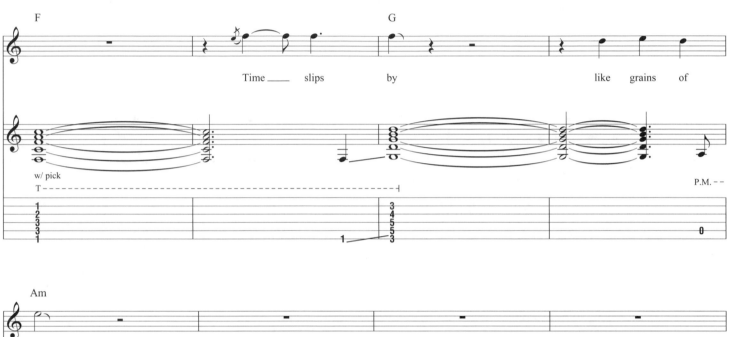

sand.

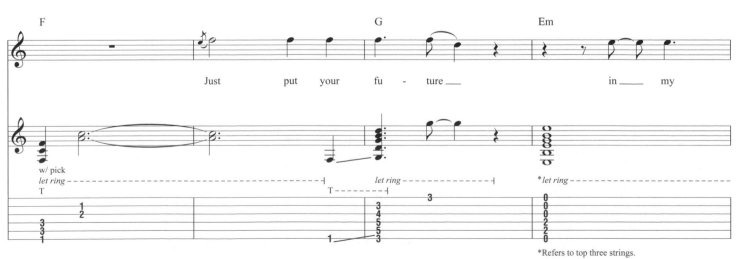

Just   put   your   fu - ture ____   in ____ my

*Refers to top three strings.

174

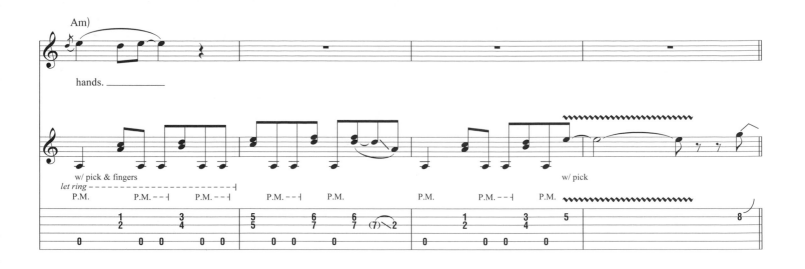

Guitar Solo

*Gtr. 3: w/ Rhy. Fig. 3 (2 times)

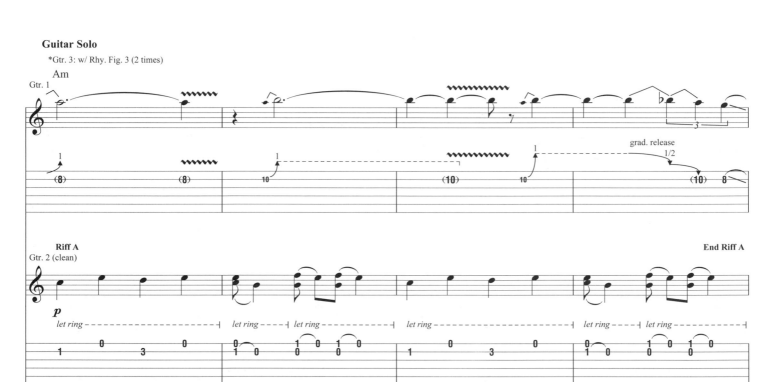

*Gtr. 3 (slight dist.) played ***mp***.

Gtr. 2: w/ Riff A

**Refers to 4th string only.

*Push down on string behind nut.

Chorus

Tell me why, ___ tell me why you look_ so

sad. _____

Time ___ slips by _____ like grains of ___

___ sand.

Just put_ your fu- ture ___ in _____ my

Gtr. 1: w/ Rhy. Fig. 1
Gtr. 2: w/ Riff A
Gtr. 3: w/ Rhy. Fig. 3 (2 times)

Am

hands. _____

Breakdown

Gtr. 1: w/ Rhy. Fig. 3 (2 times)   Gtrs. 2 & 3 tacet

Am

Gtr. 2

Gtr. 3

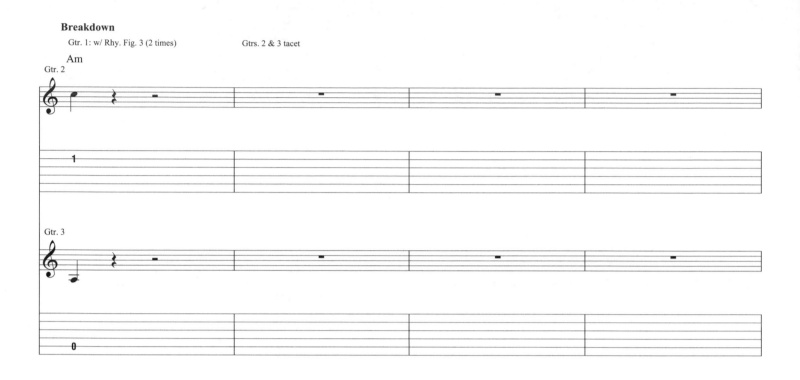

D.S. al Coda

Gtr. 1

P.M.   P.M. - - -   P.M. - - -   P.M. - - -

⊕ Coda

G

-er   if   I   can.

let ring - - - - - - - - - - - - - - - -

grad. bend

1 hold bend

178

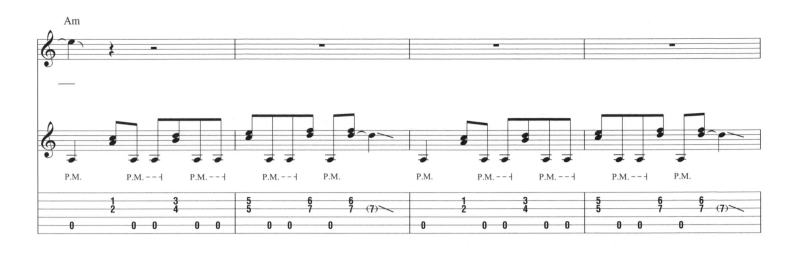

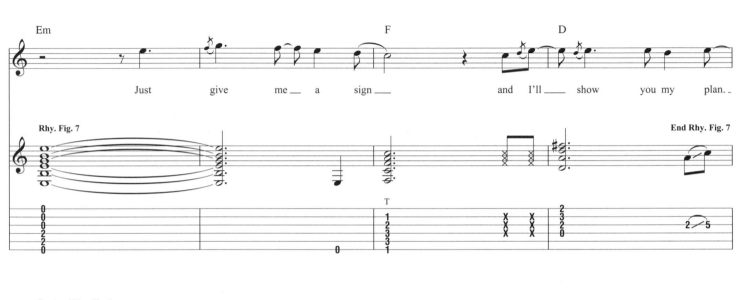

Just give me a sign ___ and I'll ___ show you my plan. ___

Just show me a smile ___ and I'll ___ show you my plan. ___

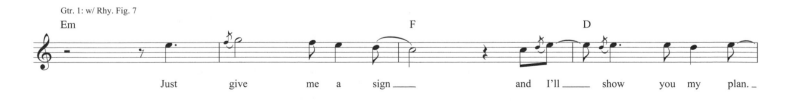

Just give me a sign ___ and I'll ___ show you my plan. ___

N.C. (Am)

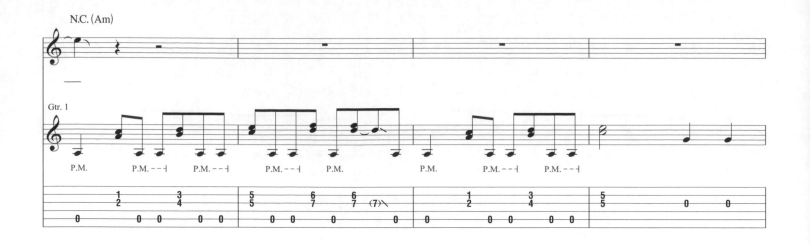

Gtr. 1

P.M.   P.M.   P.M.   P.M.   P.M.   P.M.   P.M.

Outro-Guitar Solo

Gtr. 2: w/ Riff A (till fade)
Gtr. 3: w/ Rhy. Fig. 3 (till fade)

N.C.   Am

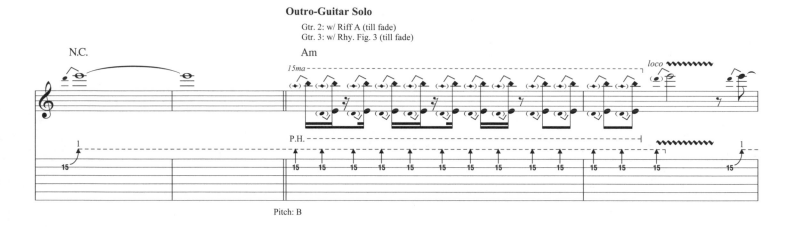

P.H.

Pitch: B

semi-
P.H.

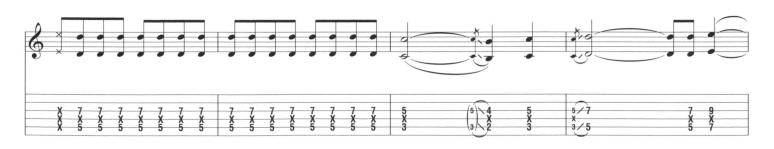

*Refers to 5th string only.

*All notes except those on 1st string which are stopped by middle finger.

from George Thorogood & The Destroyers - *George Thorogood & The Destroyers*

One Bourbon, One Scotch, One Beer

Words and Music by John Lee Hooker

Intro
Fast ♩ = 156

*E7

Gtr. 1 (dist.)

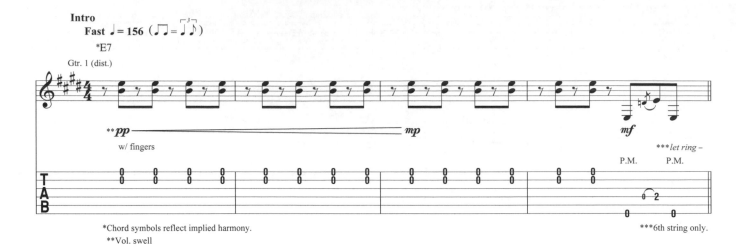

*Chord symbols reflect implied harmony.
**Vol. swell

***6th string only.

Verse

Spoken: 1. Wanna tell you a story · · · 'bout the house-rent blues.

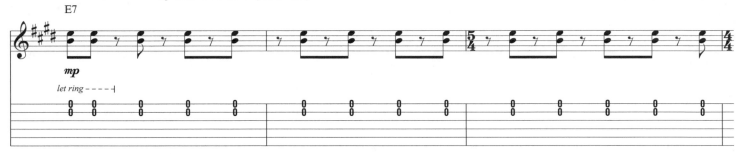

I come home one Friday,

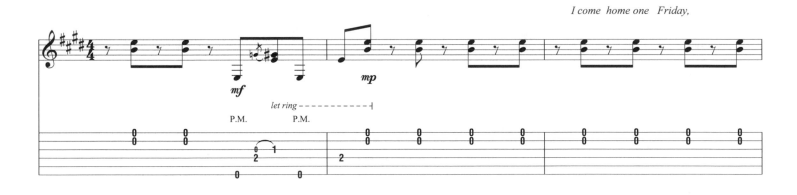

had to tell the landlady I done lost my job.

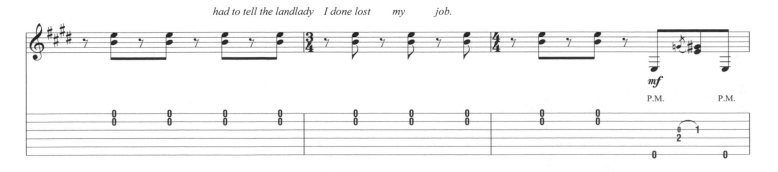

She said, "That don't confront me,   long as I   get

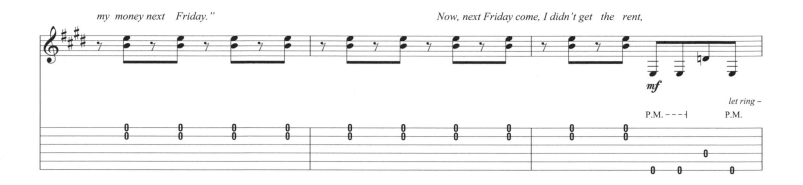

my money next   Friday."   Now, next Friday come, I didn't get   the   rent,

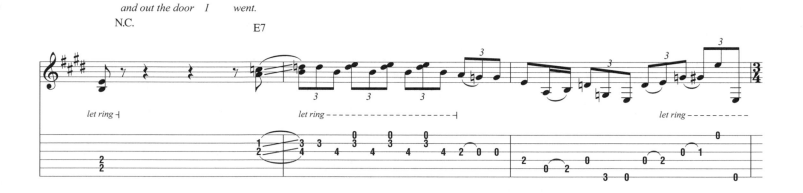

and out the door   I   went.
N.C.   E7

Verse
E7

2. So I   goes   to the   landlady

183

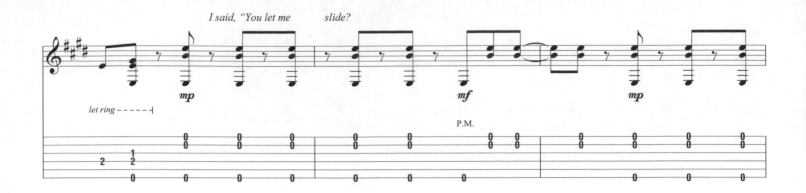

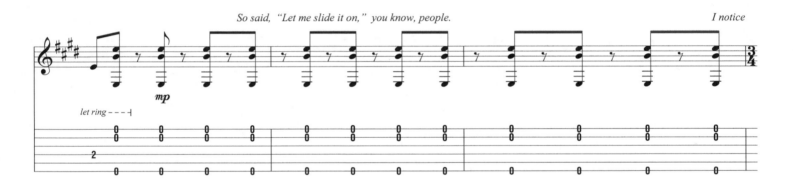

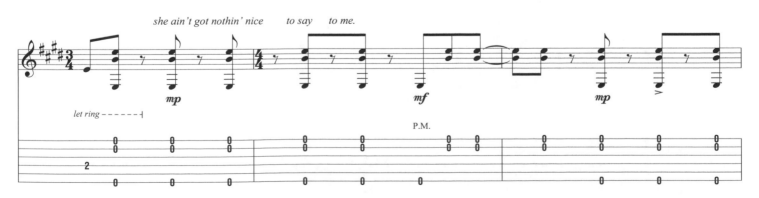

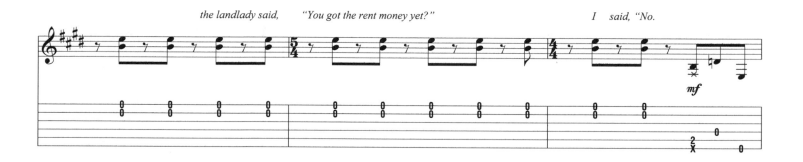

standing on a corner,   leaning up against a post."   I said, "But I'm

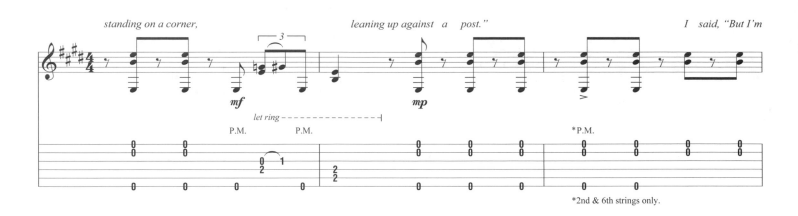

*2nd & 6th strings only.

tired,   I've been walking all day."

She said, "That don't confront me,   long as I get my money next

Friday."   Now next Friday   come, I didn't have the rent,

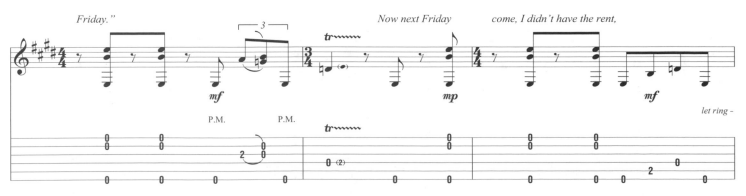

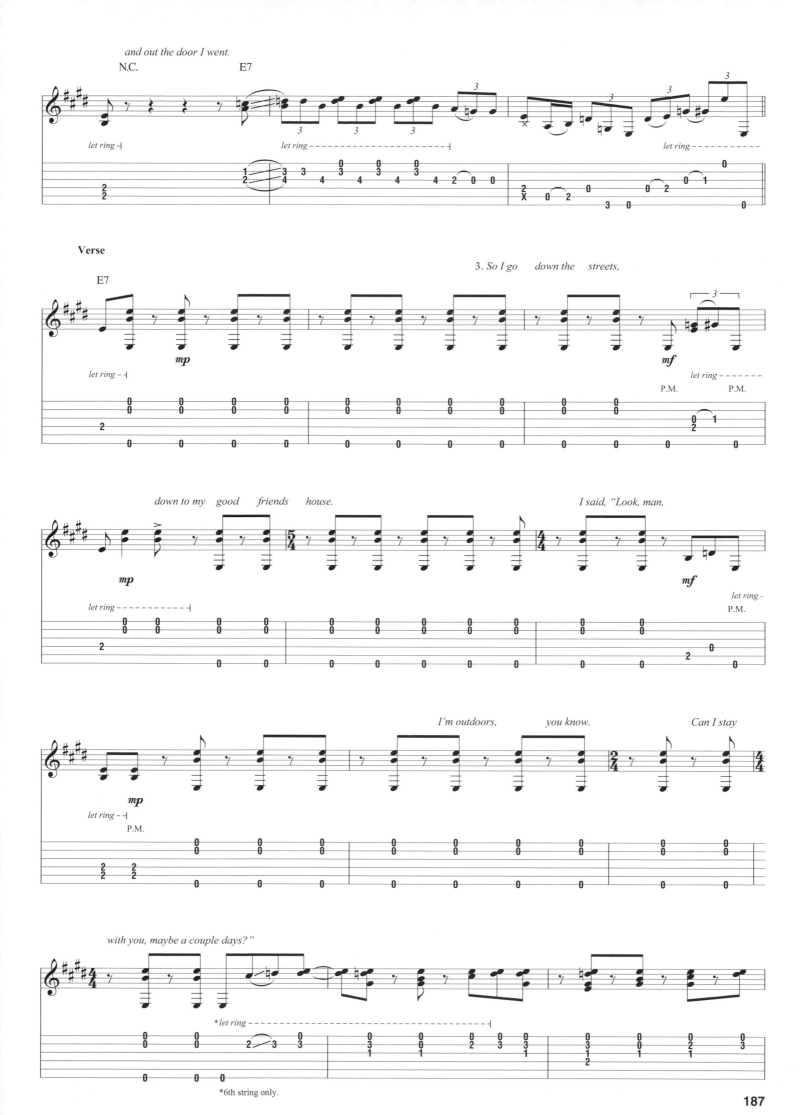

and out the door I went.

Verse

3. So I go down the streets,

down to my good friends house.

I said, "Look, man,

I'm outdoors, you know.

you know.

Can I stay

with you, maybe a couple days?"

*6th string only.

He said, "Ah, let me go and ask my wife."

He come out of the house.   I could see in his face,   I know that was no.

He said, "Ah, I don't know, man, ah, she kinda funny, you know."

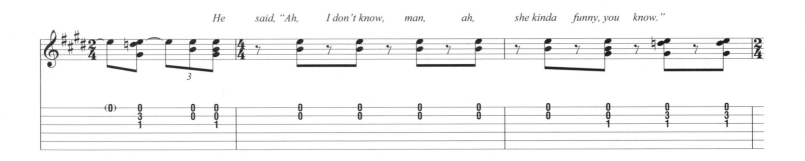

I said, "I know, everybody funny.

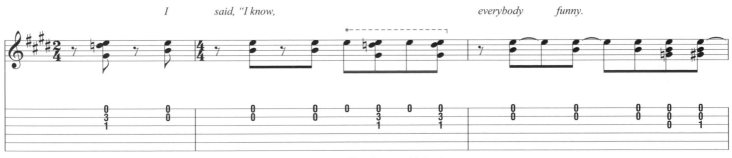

*Played as even eighth-notes.

Now you funny too."

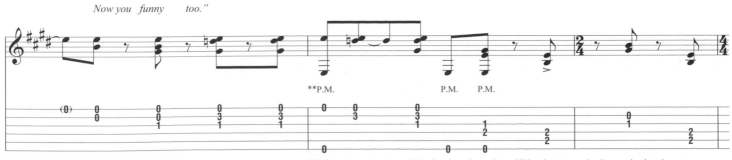

**P.M.   P.M.   P.M.

**Palm mute only notes on 6th string throughout when additional notes are simultaneously played.

So I go back home. I tell the landlady

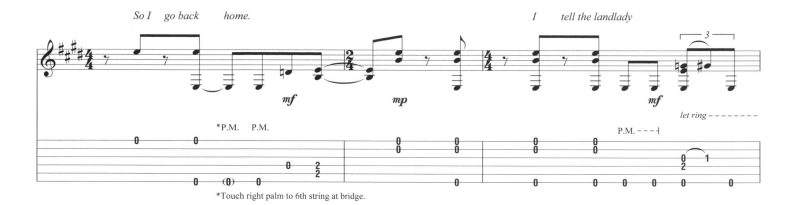

*Touch right palm to 6th string at bridge.

I got a job, I'm gonna pay the rent. She said, "Yeah?"

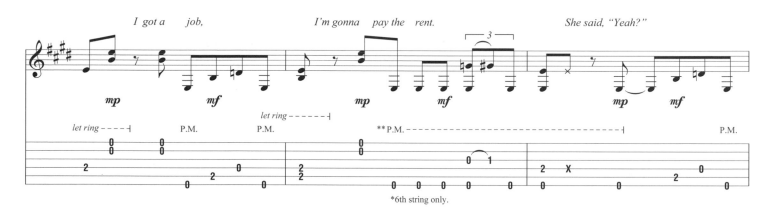

*6th string only.

I said, "Oh, yeah." And then she was so nice.

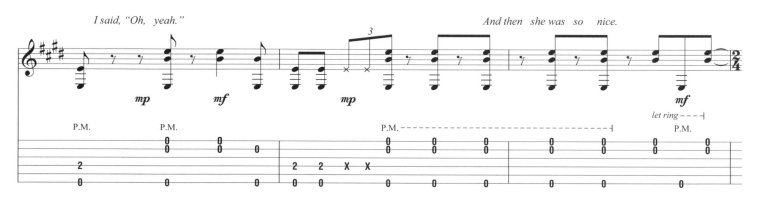

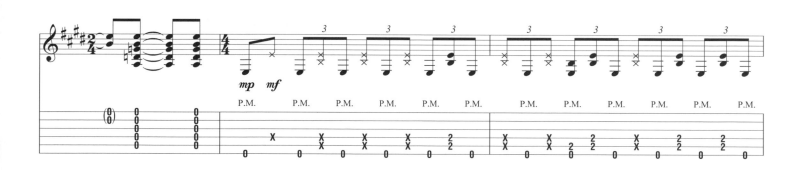

Lord, she was lovey - dovey.

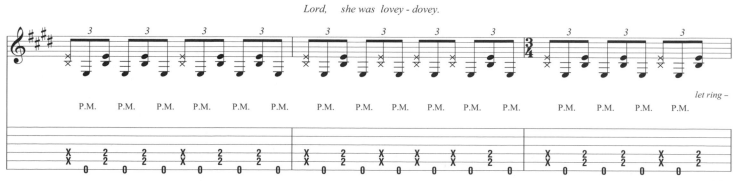

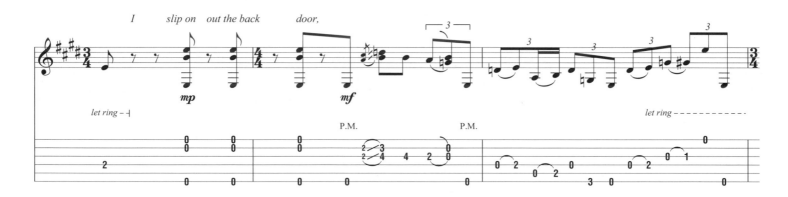

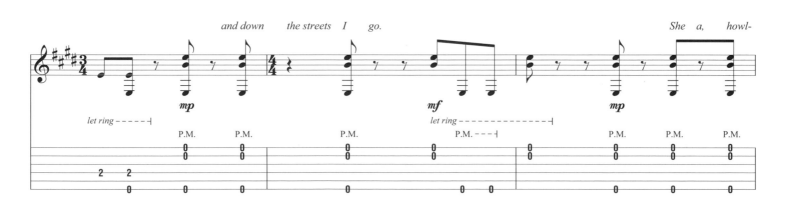

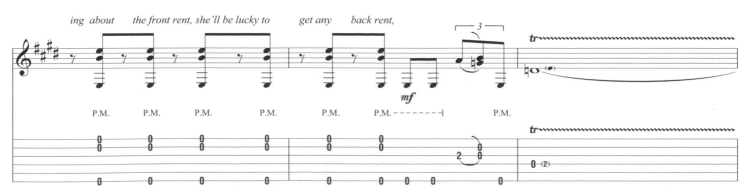

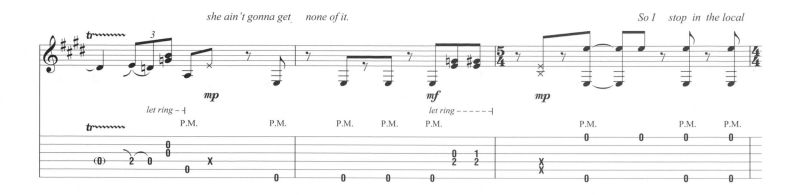

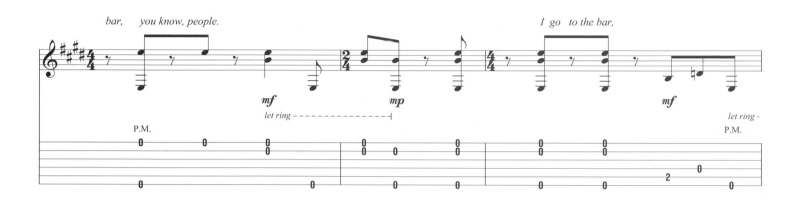

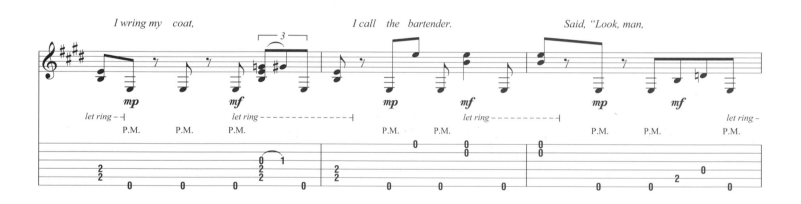

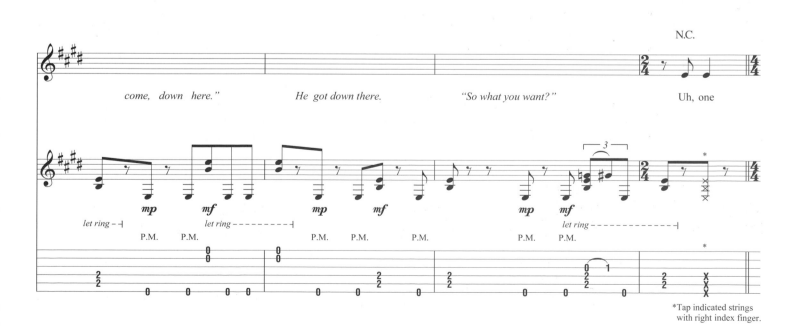

*Tap indicated strings
with right index finger.

Chorus
Slower ♩ = 135

bour bon,   uh, one   Scotch,   uh, one   beer. _____   4. Well, I

*As before

Gtr. 2 (clean)   **Riff A**   **End Riff A**

Verse

ain't seen my ba-by since I don't know when.I've been drink-ing bour-bon,whis-key,   Scotch _ and gin, _   mm. _

Riff B   **End Riff B**

Gtr. 2: w/ Riff B (8 times)

Gon-na get high, __ man, I'm gon-na get, uh, loose. Need __ me a tri-ple shot _____ of that juice.

Gtr. 1

mp   mf   mp

let ring

let ring

P.M.

Gon-na get drunk, don't you have no fear. __ I want one bour-bon, one Scotch, one beer. __ I want

mp   mf

P.M.   P.M.

let ring

Chorus

Gtr. 2: w/ Riff A

| E7 | B | | E5 | D5 | C#5 | C5 | E5 | B5 |

bour-bon, uh, one Scotch, uh, one beer. _____

let ring   let ring   let ring   let ring

Verse

Gtr. 2: w/ Riff B (21 times)

Spoken: 5. But I'm   sittin' now

E7

at   the bar.   I'm gettin' drunk,

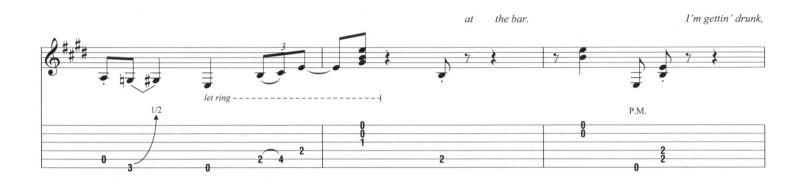

I'm   feelin' mellow.

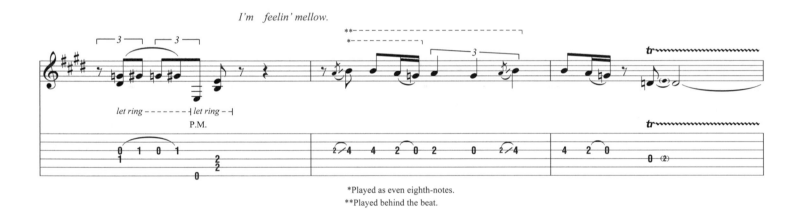

*Played as even eighth-notes.
**Played behind the beat.

I'm drinkin' bourbon,

I'm   drinkin' Scotch,   I'm   drinkin' beer.   Looked down the bar,

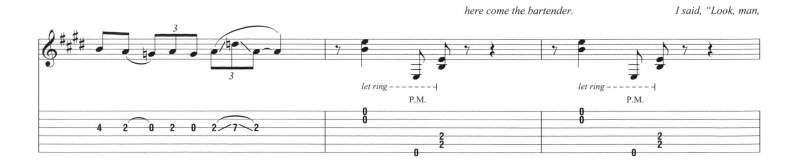

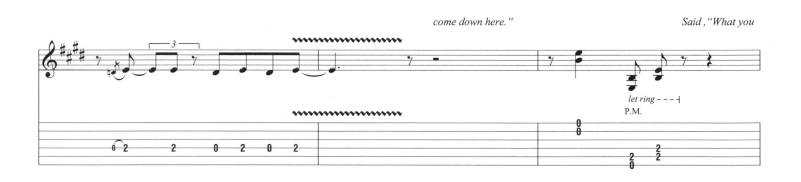

Chorus

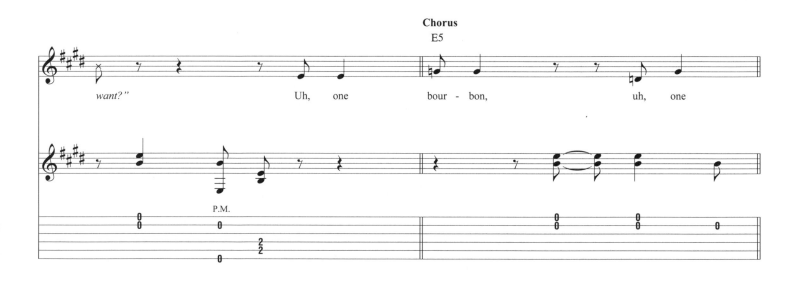

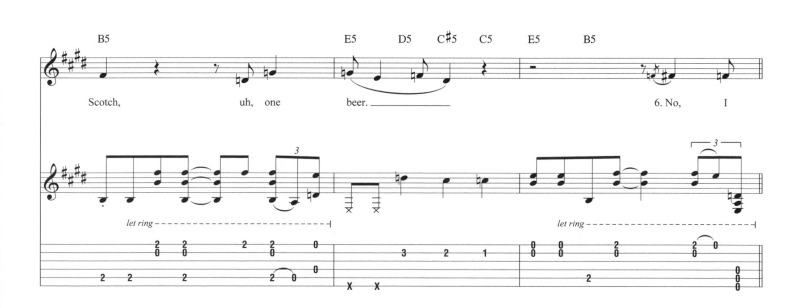

Verse

Gtr. 2: w/ Riff B (12 times)

E7

Ain't seen my ba-by since the night be-fore last. Got-ta get a drink, man, I'm gon-na get gassed.

Gon-na get high, man, I ain't had e-nough, need me a tri-ple shot of that stuff.

*Tap indicated strings with right index finger.

Gon-na get drunk, won't you lis-ten right here, I want one bour-bon, one shot and one beer. Uh, one

Chorus

Gtr. 2: w/ Riff A

E   B   E5 D5   C#5 C5   E5 B5

bour-bon, uh, one Scotch, uh, one beer, well, al - right.

196

Guitar Solo

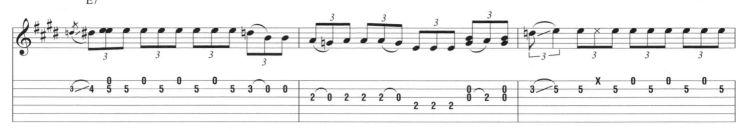

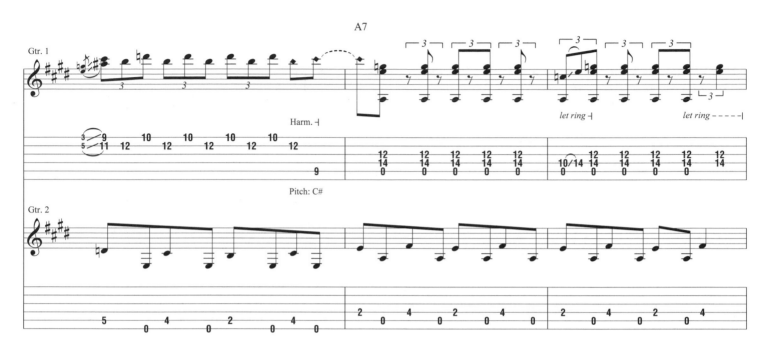

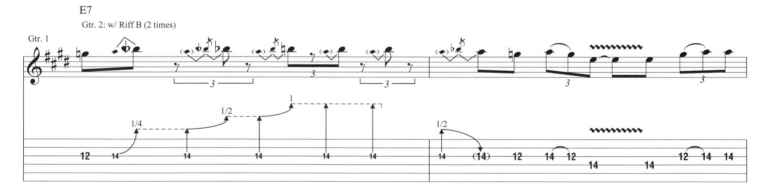

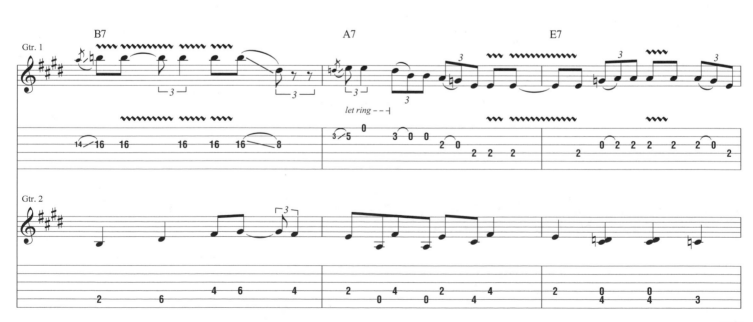

Gtr. 2: w/ Riff A (last meas.)   Gtr. 2: w/ Riff B (42 times)

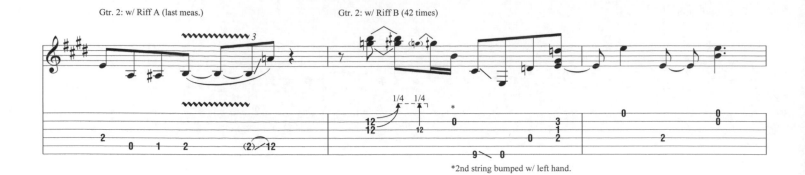

*2nd string bumped w/ left hand.

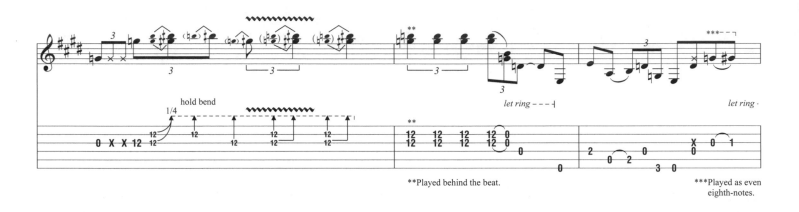

**Played behind the beat.   ***Played as even
eighth-notes.

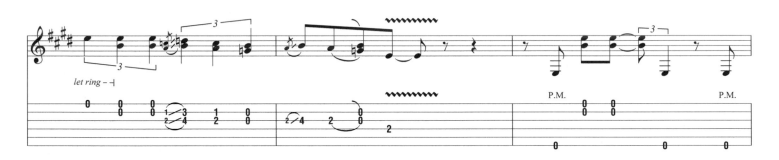

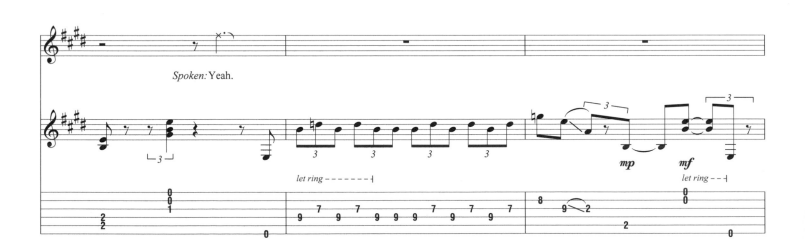

Spoken: Yeah.

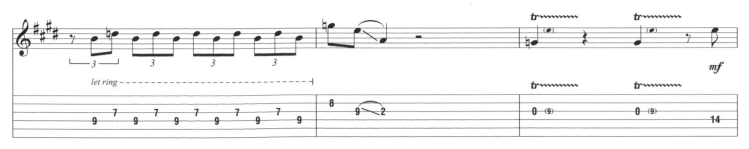

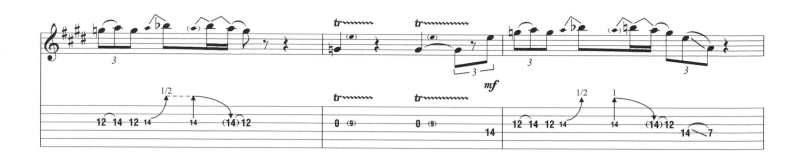

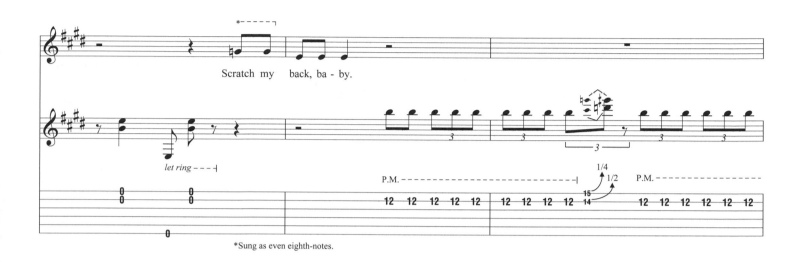

Scratch my   back, ba - by.

*Sung as even eighth-notes.

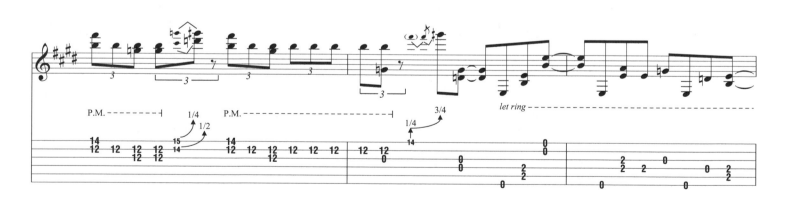

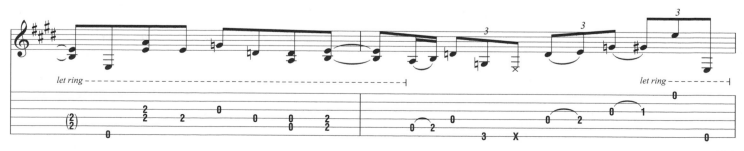

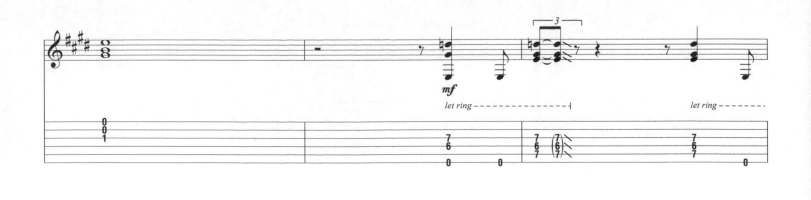

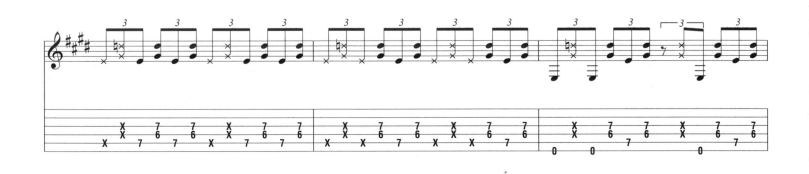

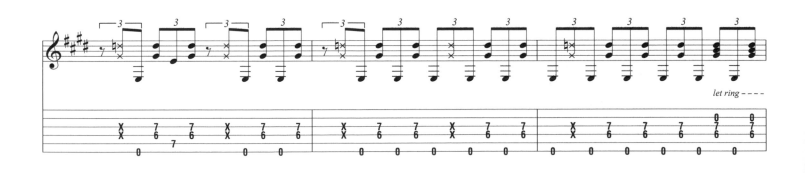

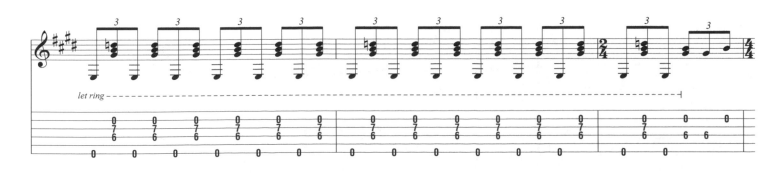

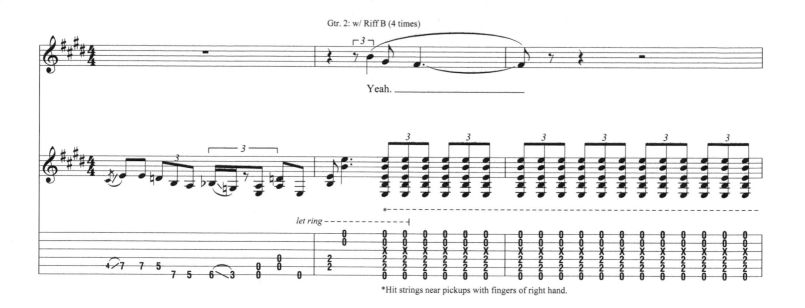

Yeah.

*Hit strings near pickups with fingers of right hand.

Verse

Gtr. 2: w/ Riff B (22 times)

Spoken: 6. *Now by this time*

E7

**Tap indicated strings with
right index finger.

I'm plenty high.   *You know when your mouth is gettin' dry*

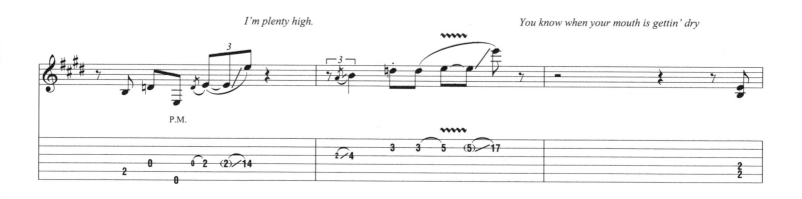

you're plenty high.   *Looked down the bar,*   *I see to my barten-*

der.   I said, "Look, man,   come down here."   He got down

there.   "So what you want this time."   I said, "Look, man,   uh,   what time is

it?"   He   said, "The clock on the wall   say   three o'clock.

Uh, last   call

for alcohol,   so what you need?"

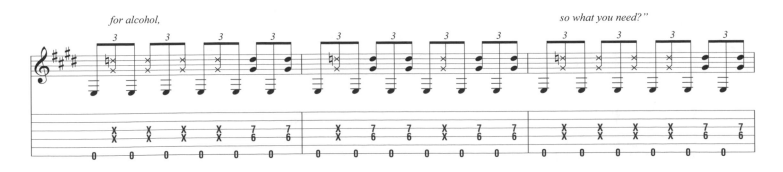

wan-na get drunk, I'm gon-na make it real clear, I want one bour-bon, one Scotch and one beer. Uh, one

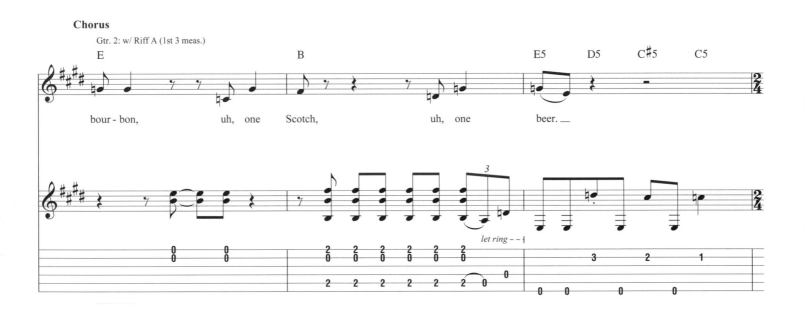

Chorus

Gtr. 2: w/ Riff A (1st 3 meas.)

E   B   E5 D5 C#5 C5

bour - bon,   uh, one Scotch,   uh, one   beer.

let ring -- ┤

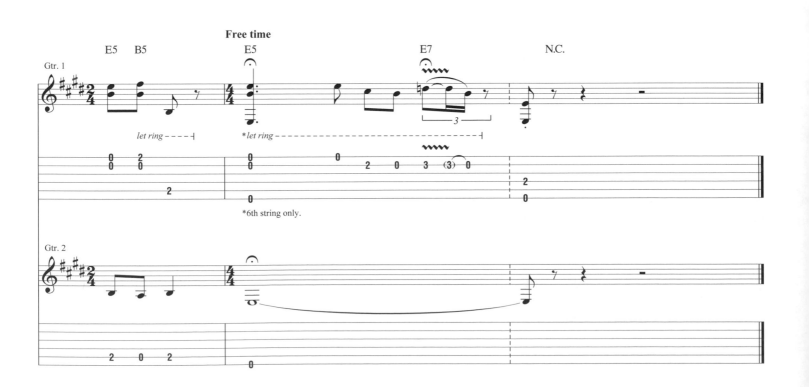

Free time

E5 B5   E5   E7   N.C.

Gtr. 1

let ring ----┤ *let ring ---------------------┤

*6th string only.

Gtr. 2

from The Allman Brothers Band - *Eat a Peach*

One Way Out

Words and Music by Willie Williamson, Elmore James and Marshall Sehorn

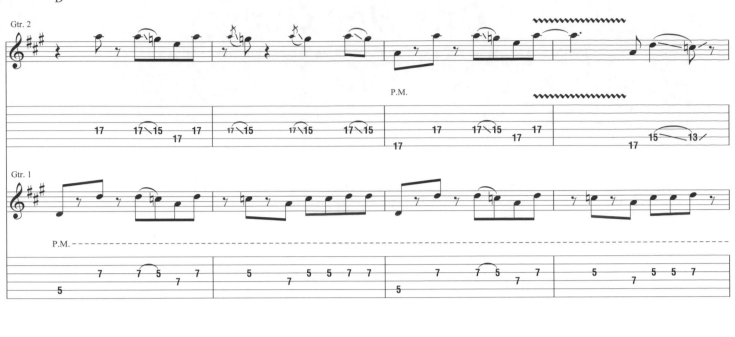

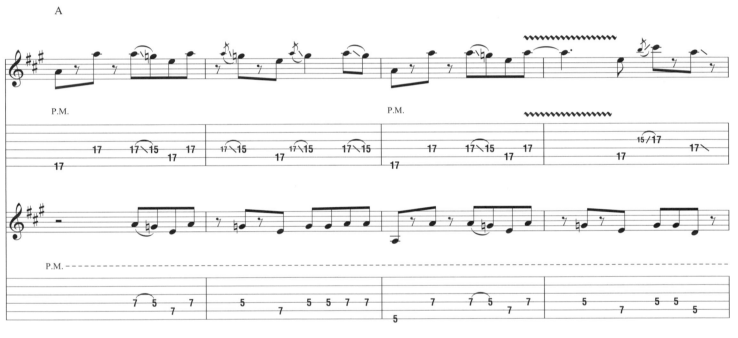

*Switch pickup selector to treble position,
w/ vol. control set to full vol.)

Guitar Solo

Rhy. Fig. 1

w/o slide

Breakdown

Gtrs. 1 & 2 tacet

Oh.   *Spoken: Put your hands together.*

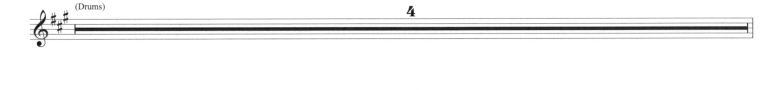

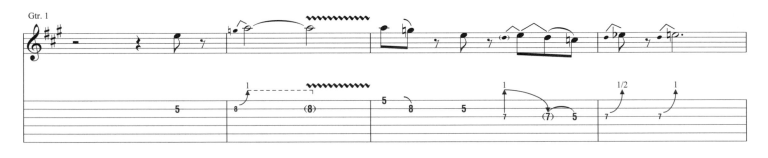

*Switch pickup selector to treble position, w/ vol. control set to full vol.

214

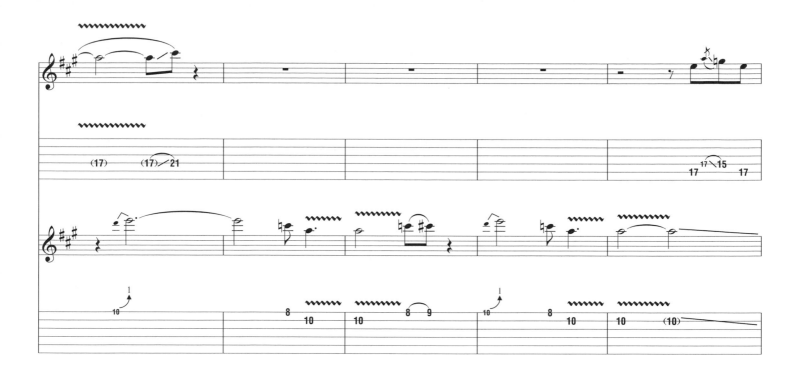

Gtr. 1 tacet

Guitar Solo

D

*Gtr. 1

P.M. --

*Switch pickup selector to rhythm position.

*Switch pickup selector to rhythm position.

216

from CRY OF LOVE - *Brother*

Peace Pipe

Written by Audley Freed and Kelly Holland

*Chord symbols reflect implied harmony.

**Gtr. 2 (dist.), played *mf*.

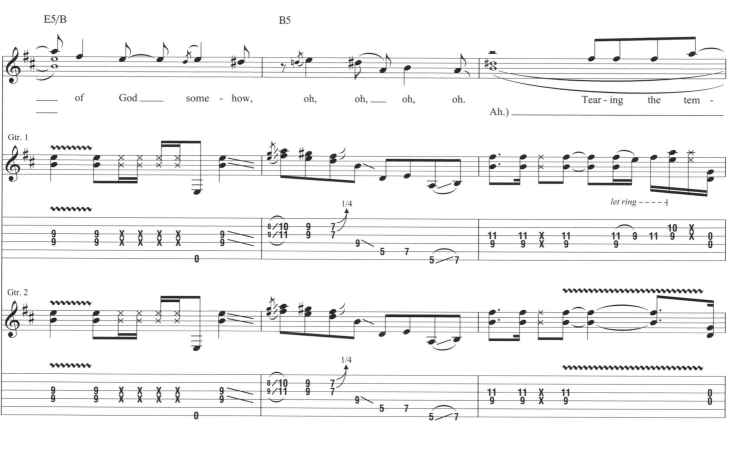

of God ___ some - how, oh, oh, ___ oh, oh.
(Ah.) ___ Tear - ing the tem-

Chorus

- ple down. ___ Burn down the sa - cred ground, tear - ing the tem - ple down,

To Coda ⊕

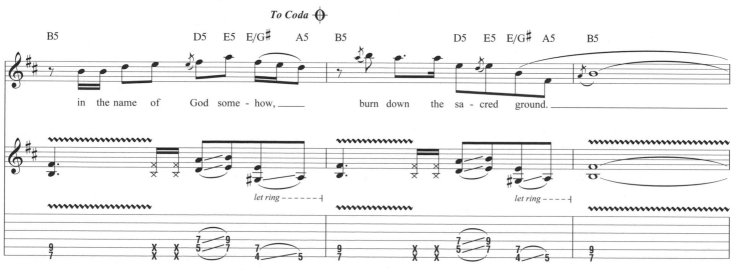

in the name of God some - how, ___ burn down the sa - cred ground. ___

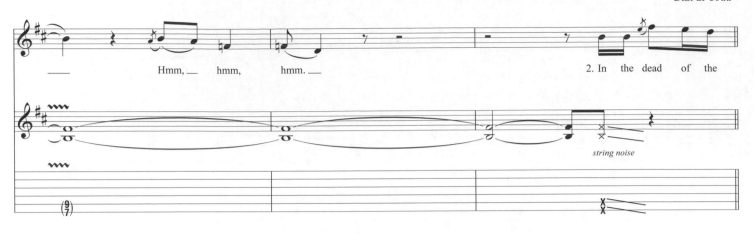

Hmm, ___ hmm, ___ hmm. ___

2. In the dead of the

string noise

⊕ Coda

Bridge

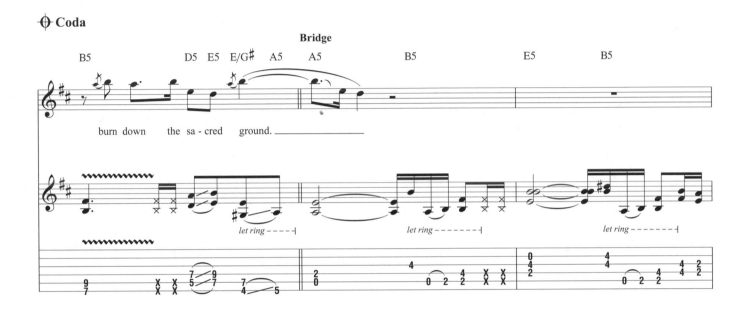

B5   D5   E5   E/G♯   A5   A5   B5   E5   B5

burn down   the sa - cred   ground. ___

let ring   *let ring*   *let ring*

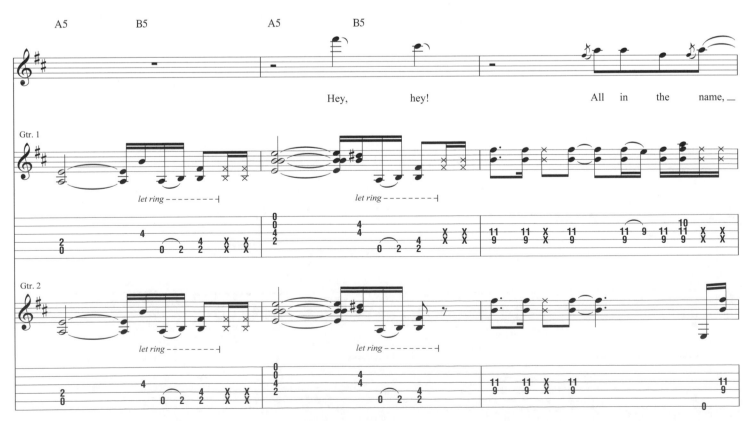

A5   B5   A5   B5

Hey,   hey!   All in   the name, ___

Gtr. 1

let ring   *let ring*

Gtr. 2

let ring   *let ring*

*Bass plays E.

all in the name, _____ yeah!

Guitar Solo

Gtrs. 1 & 2 tacet

Gtr. 3 (dist.)

Gtr. 2

Gtr. 1
divisi

Gtr. 3

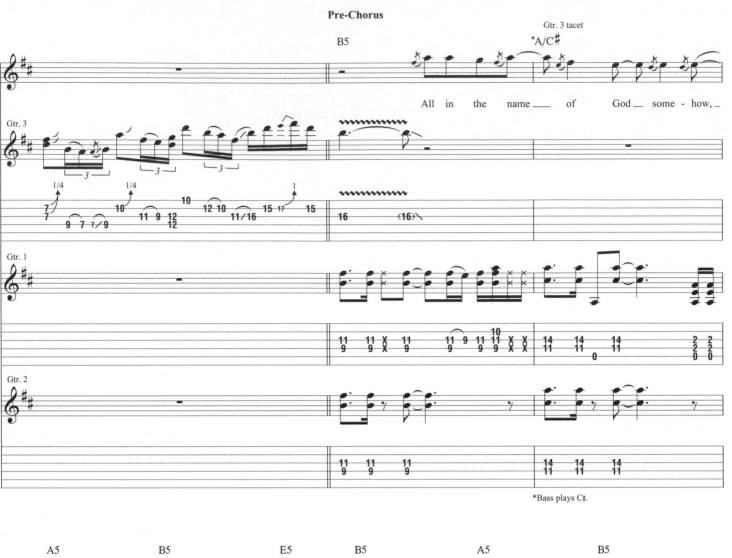

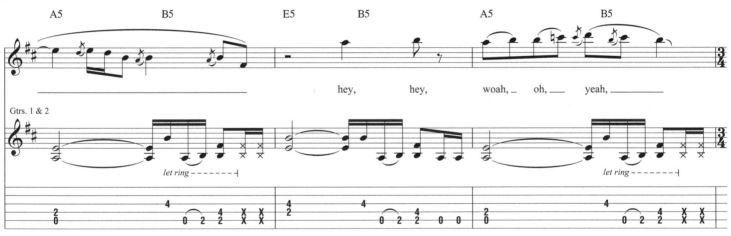

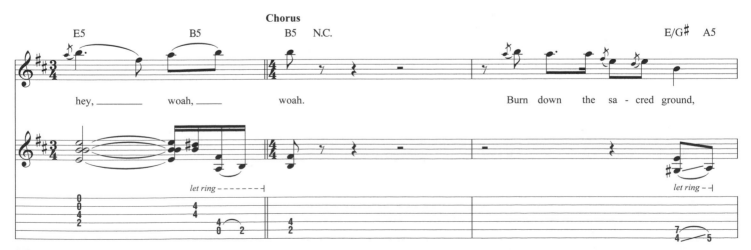

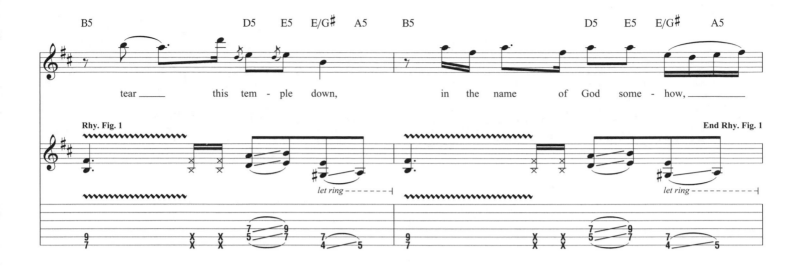

tear _____ this tem - ple down, in the name of God some - how, _____

Rhy. Fig. 1

End Rhy. Fig. 1

let ring -------| let ring ----------|

Gtrs. 1 & 2: w/ Rhy. Fig. 1

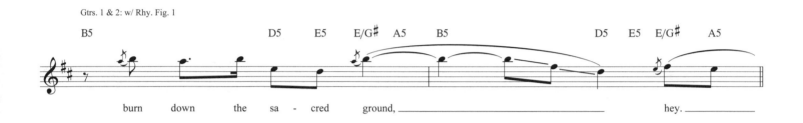

burn down the sa - cred ground, _____ hey. _____

Outro-Guitar Solo

Gtrs. 1 & 2: w/ Rhy. Fig. 1 (till fade)

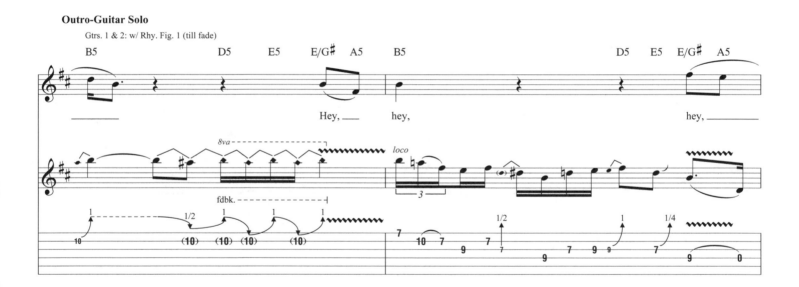

Hey, _____ hey, hey, _____

8va ----------| loco

fdbk. --------|

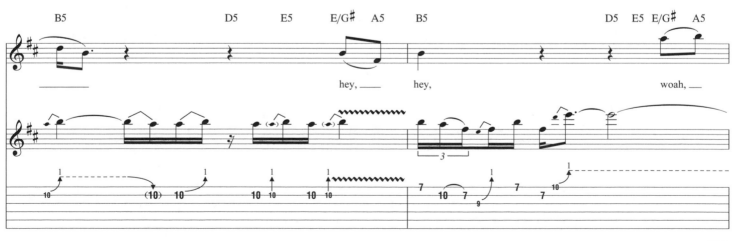

_____ hey, _____ hey, woah, _____

from Pat Travers - *Makin' Magic*

Rock n Roll Susie

Words and Music by Pat Travers

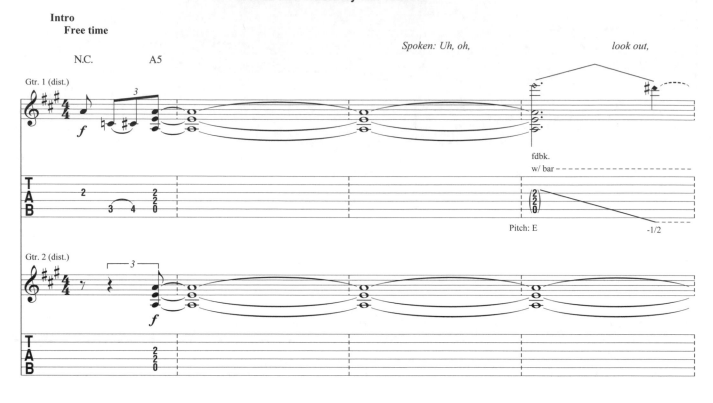

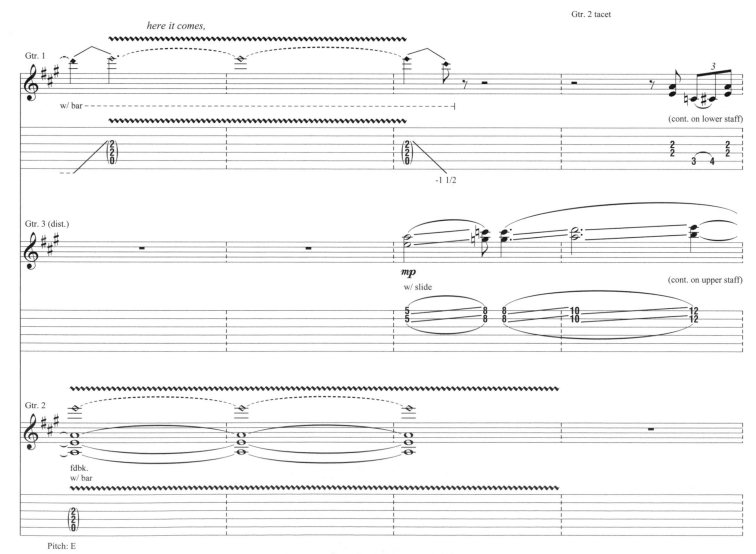

1. I'm ___ gon-na

End Riff A

End Riff A1

Verse
A5

rock,   gon-na rock ___ and   roll ___ to - night. ___   I'm ___ gon-na   free, ___

*Gtrs. 1 & 2   **Rhy. Fig. 1**

*Composite arrangement

F   A5   E5

___ gon-na show ___ my   soul ___ the   light. _____   I'm ___ gon-na

Verse

shake, _ shake our heads _ a - round. _

Gtr. 3

Gtrs. 1 & 2

Gtr. 3 tacet

Get - tin' down, _ to that raunch - y sound. _

Interlude
Gtrs. 1 & 2: w/ Riffs A & A1

N.C.(A5)

Look out!

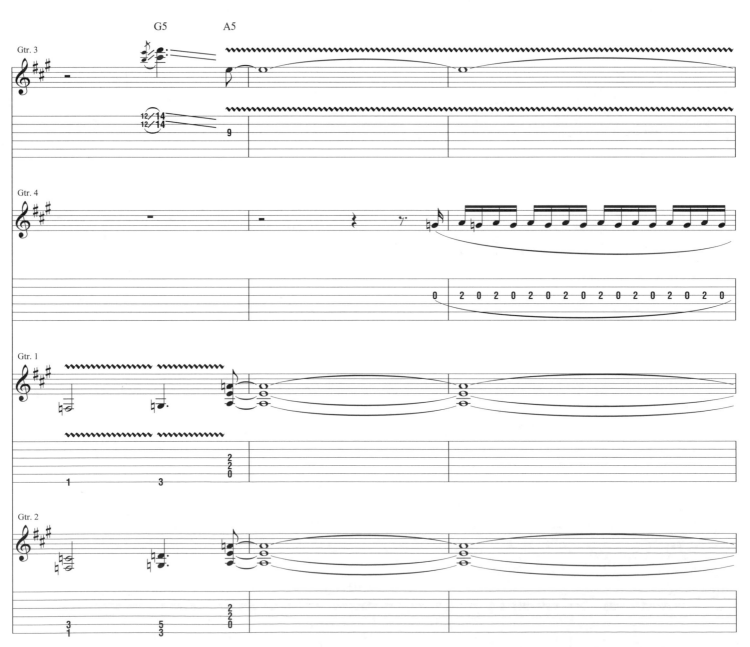

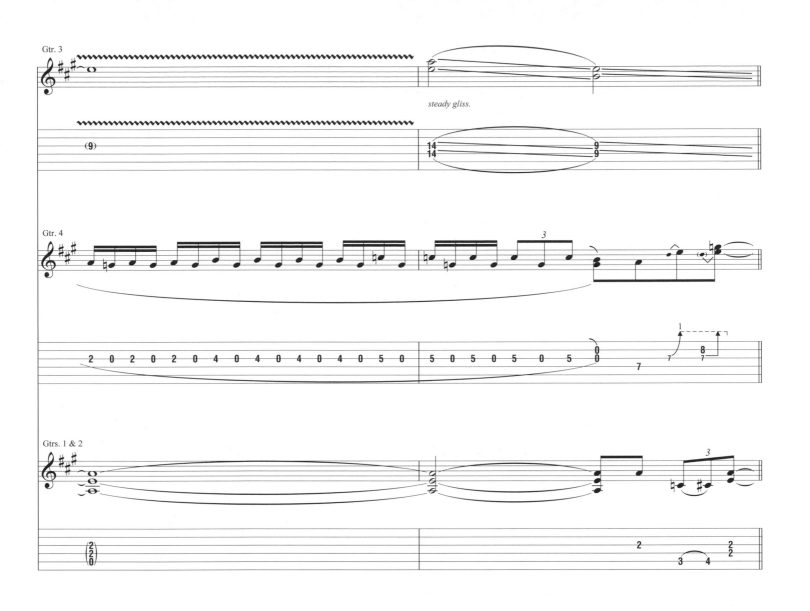

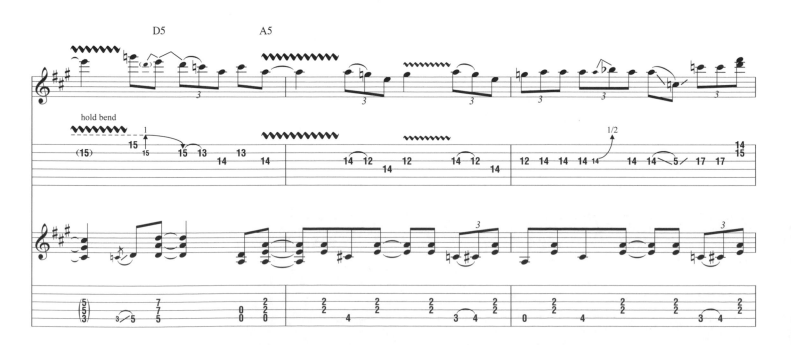

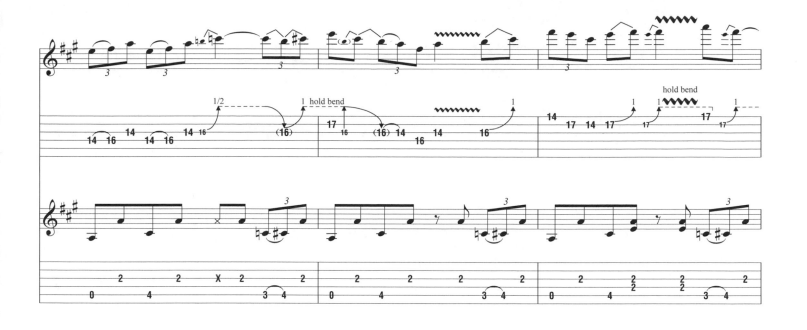

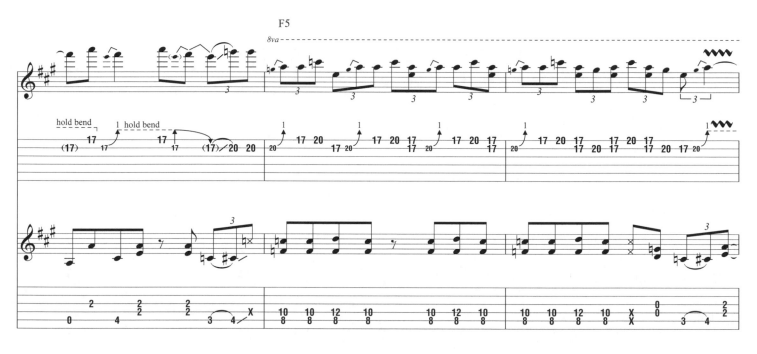

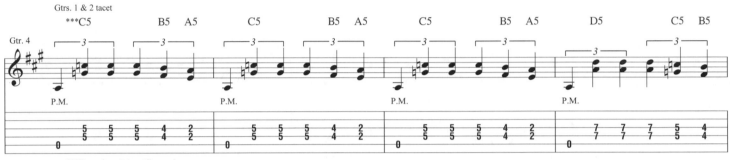

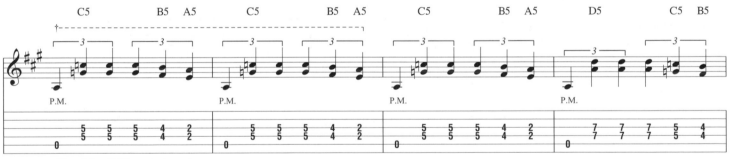

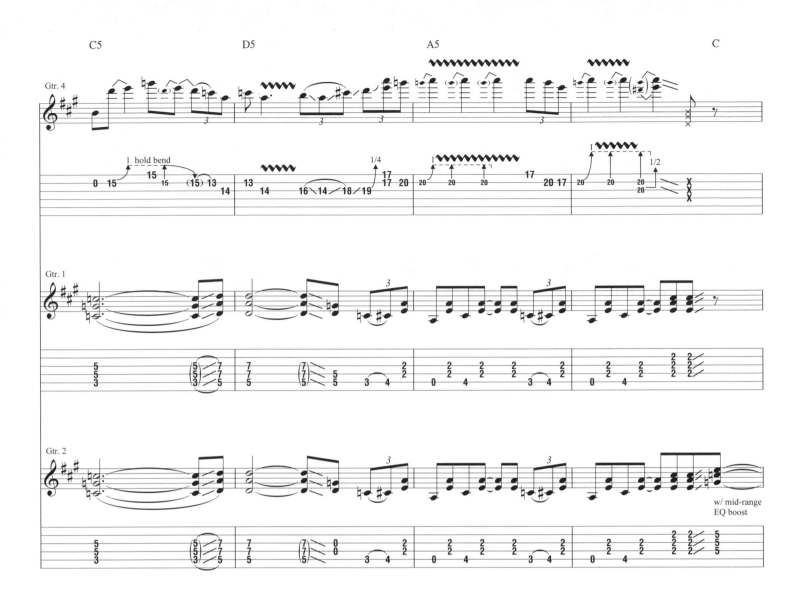

239

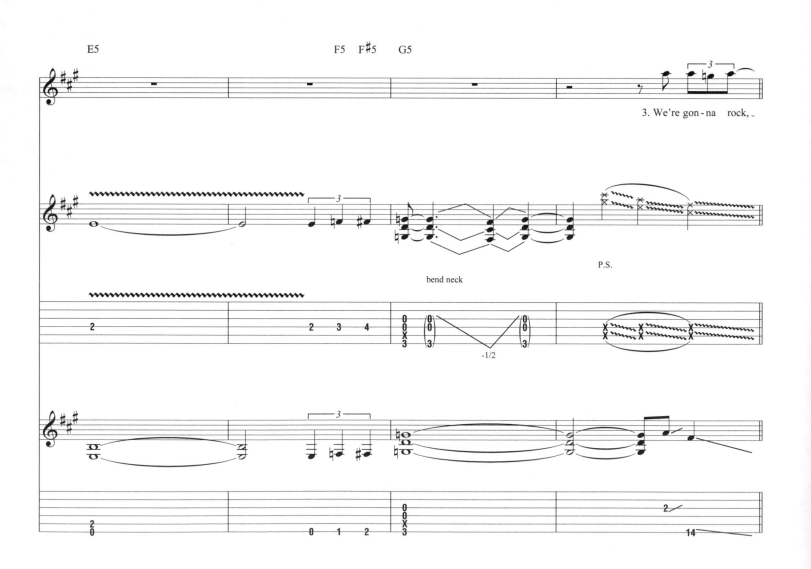

know it's gon-na be al - right? _____ Al - right. _

Outro
Gtrs. 1 & 2: w/ Riffs A & A1
Gtr. 4 tacet

N.C.(A5)

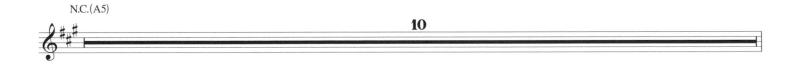

10

Free time

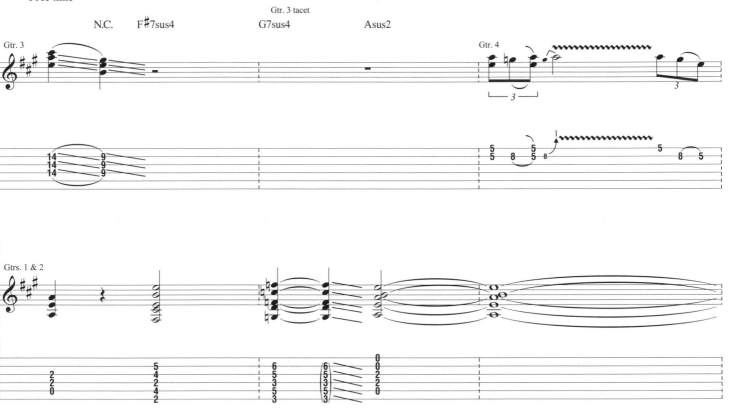

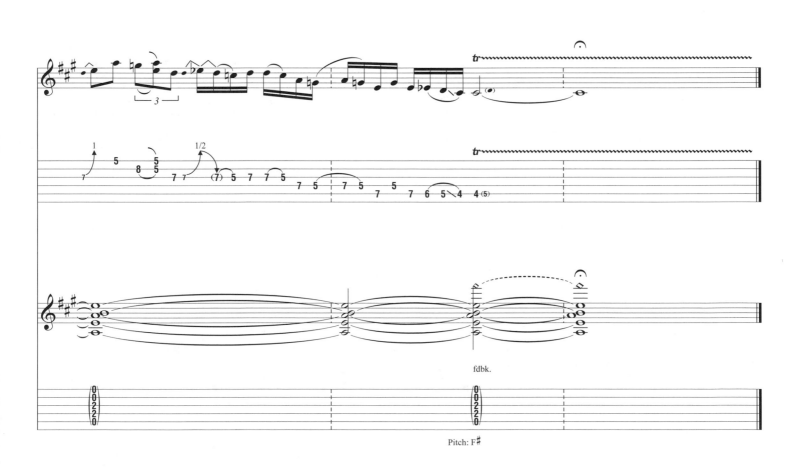

from Cream - *Disraeli Gears*

Swlabr

Words and Music by Jack Bruce and Pete Brown

Chorus

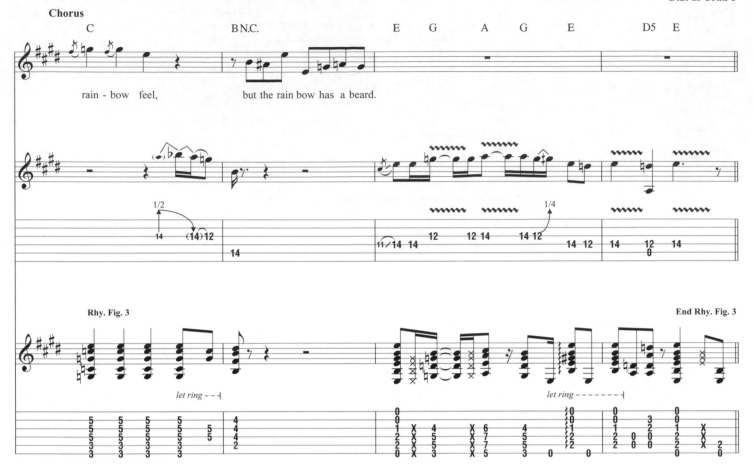

rain - bow feel, but the rain bow has a beard.

⊕ Coda 1

Chorus

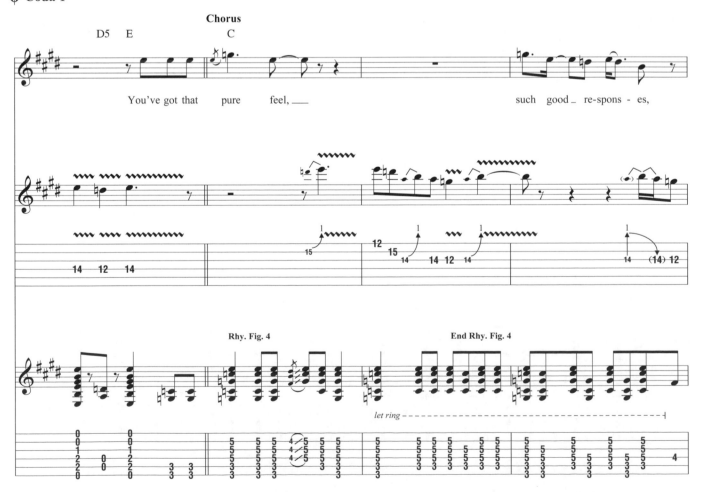

You've got that pure feel, ___ such good_ re-spons - es,

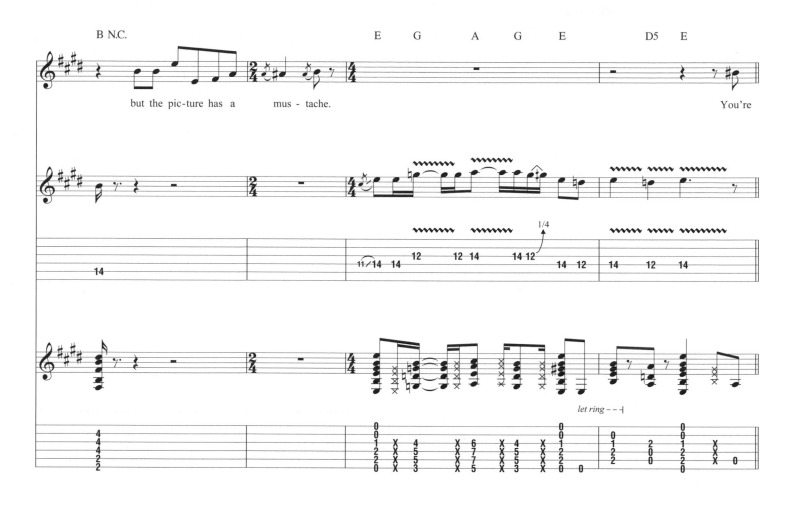

but the pic-ture has a mus - tache. You're

Bridge

com-ing to me with that soul - ful __ look on your face. ___

Guitar Solo

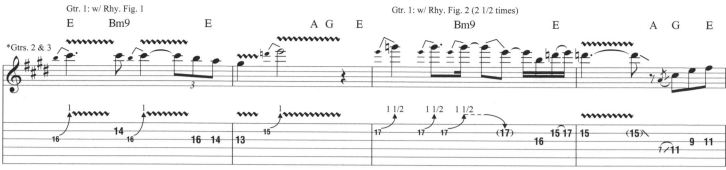

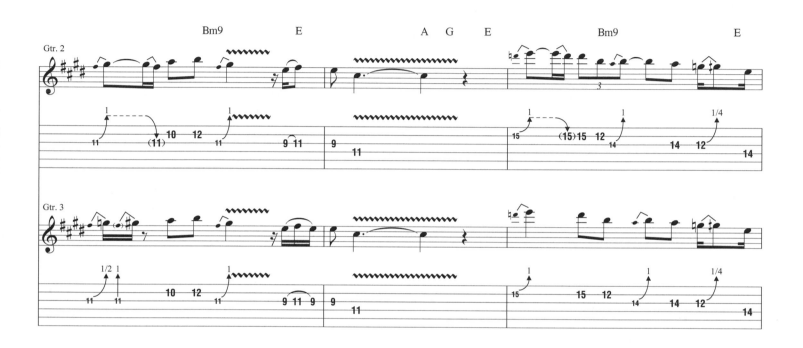

You're

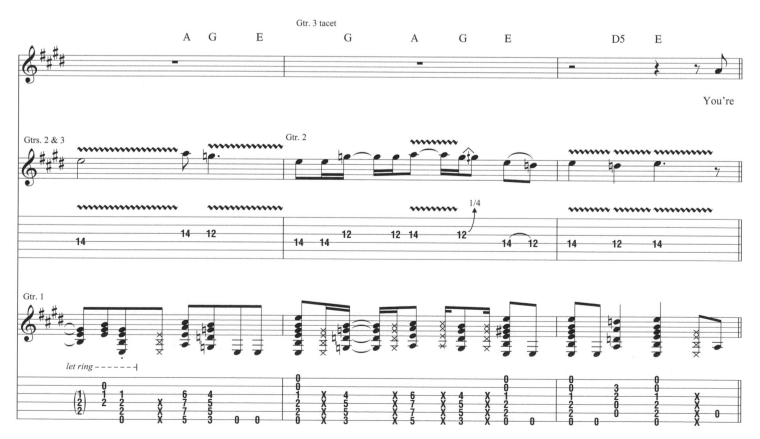

⊕ **Coda 2**

Chorus

Gtr. 1: w/ Rhy. Fig. 4 (2 times)

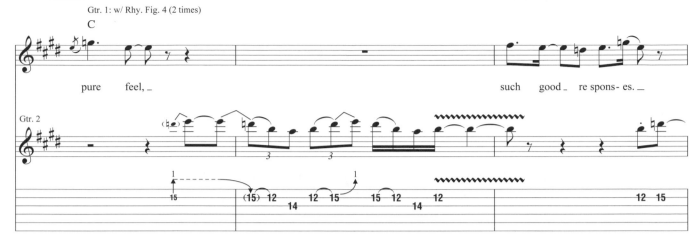

pure feel, ___ such good ___ re spons- es. ___

Gtr. 1: w/ Rhy. Fig. 3

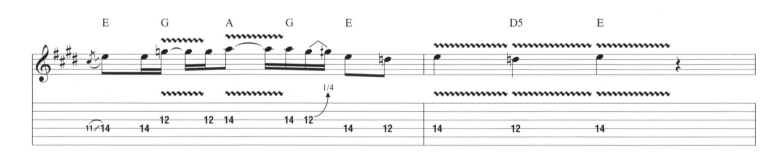

Got ___ that rain - bow feel, ___ but the rain-bow has a beard.

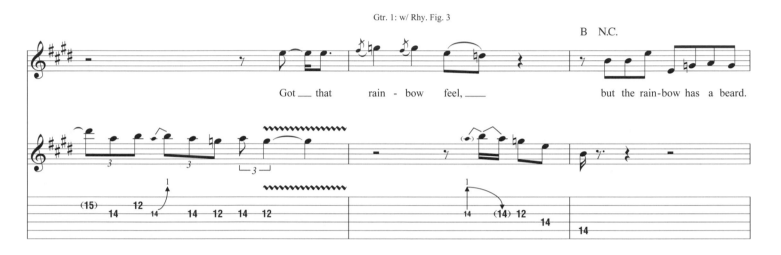

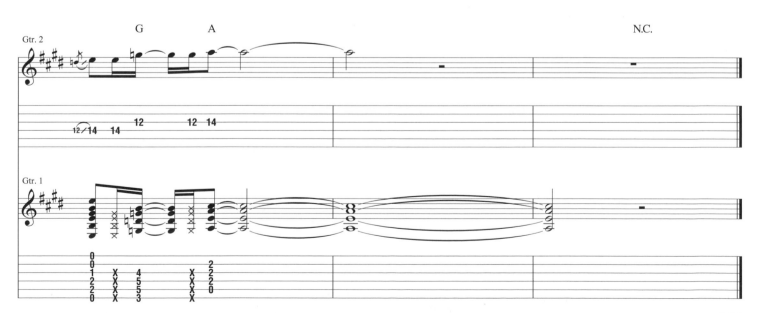

Traveling Riverside Blues

Words and Music by Robert Johnson

*Gtr. 1: Open G tuning:
(low to high) D-G-D-G-B-D

Intro
Moderately ♩ = 120

***G

**Gtr. 1
(12-str. elec.)

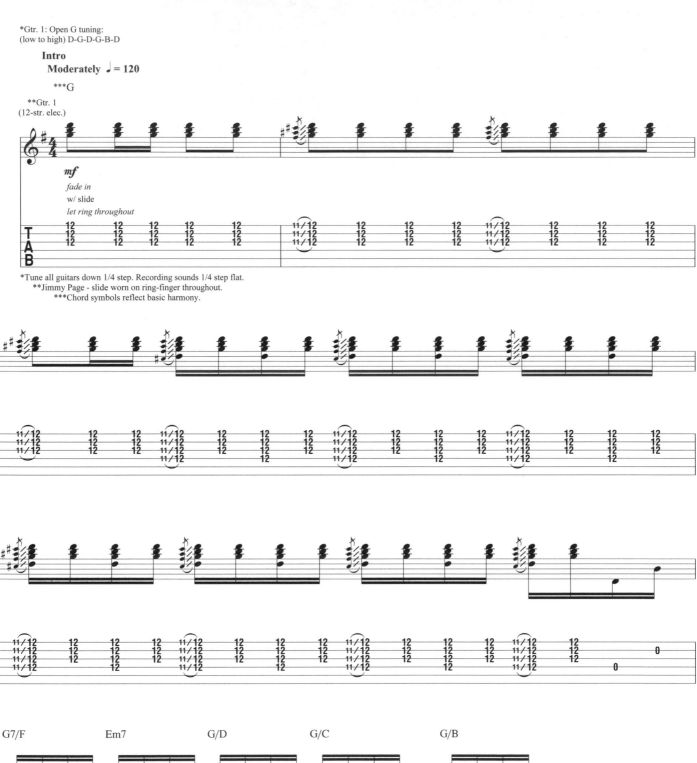

*Tune all guitars down 1/4 step. Recording sounds 1/4 step flat.
**Jimmy Page - slide worn on ring-finger throughout.
***Chord symbols reflect basic harmony.

G7/F   Em7   G/D   G/C   G/B

w/o slide

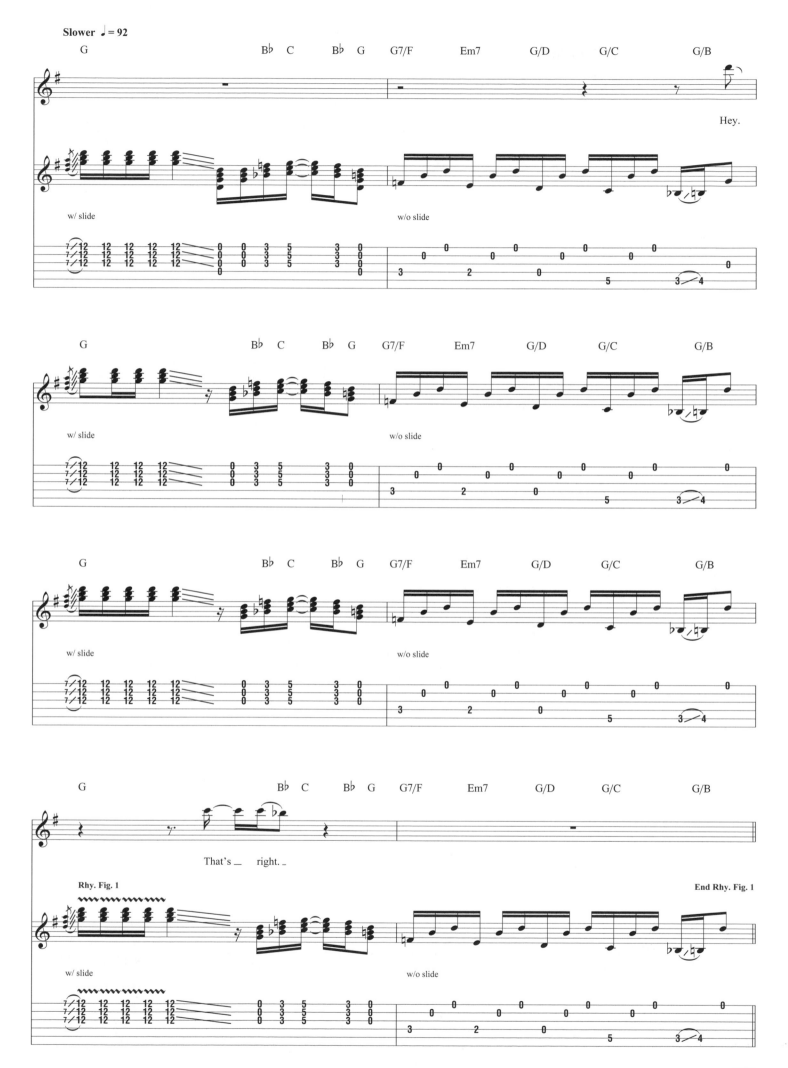

Chorus

Verse

Interlude

Guitar Solo

*Jimmy Page - studio overdub.

Gtr. 1: w/ Rhy. Fig. 3

C7

Spoken: Ah.

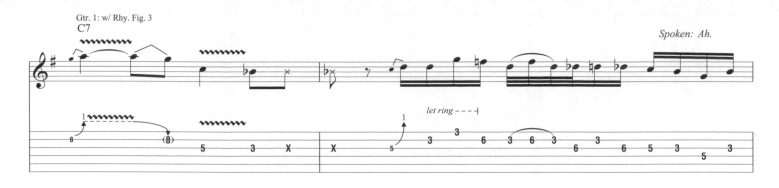

Gtr. 1: w/ Rhy. Fig. 2 (2 times)

G7

Why don't you come in my kitchen?

D7   C7

Gtr. 2

Gtr. 1

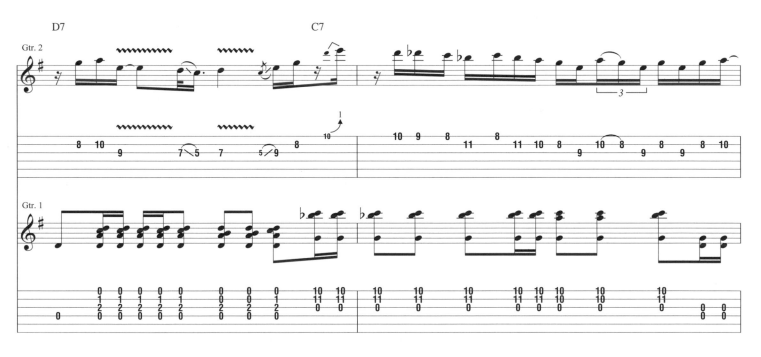

G   G7/F   Em7   G/E♭

w/ pick & fingers

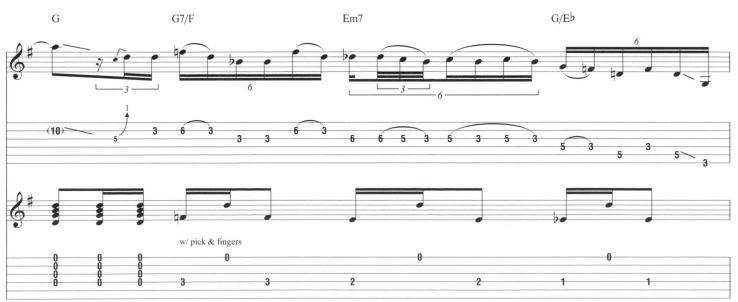

True Lies

Words and Music by Kenny Wayne Shepherd and Danny Tate

*Chord symbols reflect implied tonality.

Verse

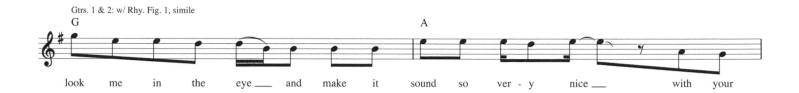

look me in the eye ___ and make it sound so ver - y nice ___ with your

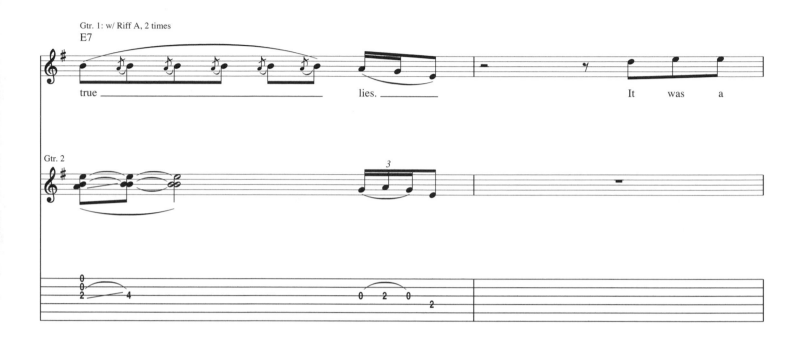

true _____ lies. _____ It was a

clev - er dis - guise ___ but, girl, ___ I'm get - tin' wise _____ to your

true _____ lies. _____ Well, ___ you been

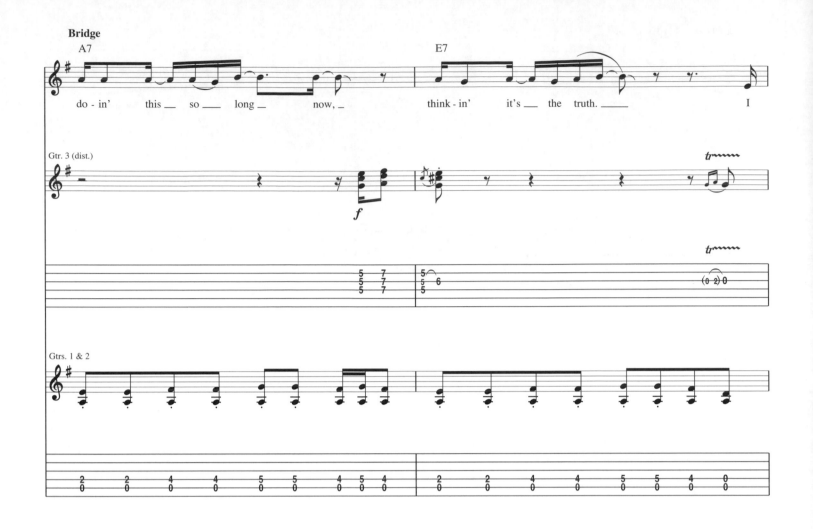

do - in' this __ so __ long __ now, __ think - in' it's __ the truth. _____ I

guess it don't __ seem wrong _____ if it ain't be - in' done to you. _____

You've, got-ta lot to learn, _ ba - by, you can't keep it down. ____ When the

string noise

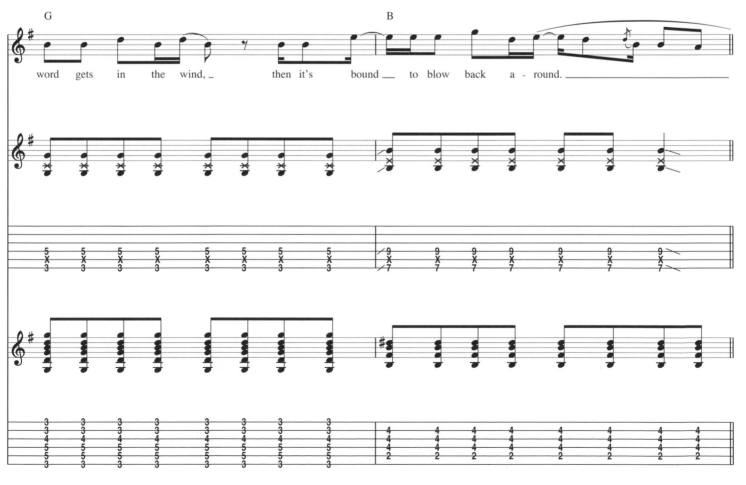

word gets in the wind, _ then it's bound __ to blow back a - round. _____ When the

Guitar Solo

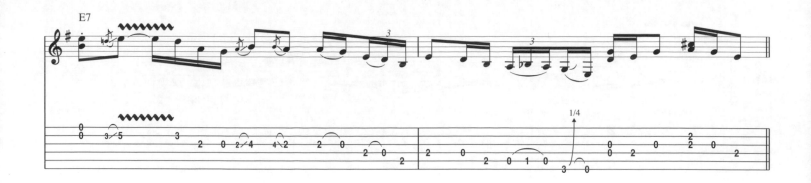

Verse

Gtr. 3 tacet

E7

3. Girl, ___ can you give me a rea - son?   I bet you don't e - ven know why. ___

Gtr. 1

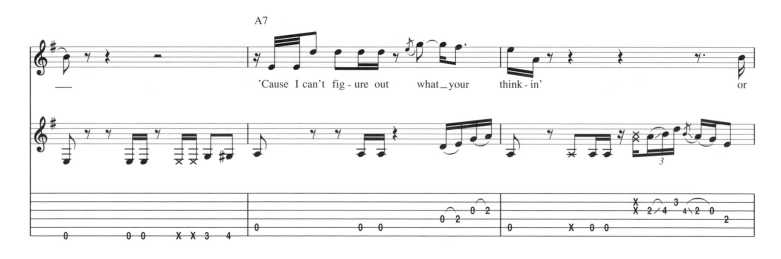

'Cause I can't fig - ure out   what ___ your   think - in'   or

E7

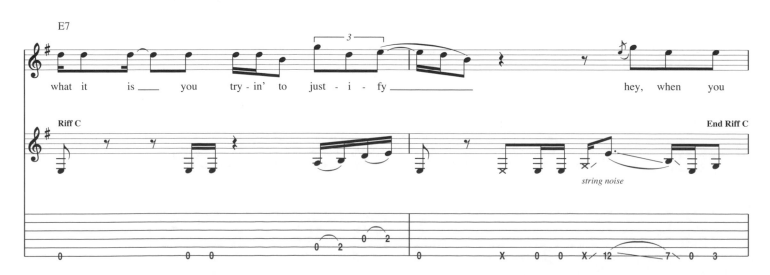

what it   is ___ you   try - in' to   just - i - fy _____   hey, when   you

Riff C   **End Riff C**

string noise

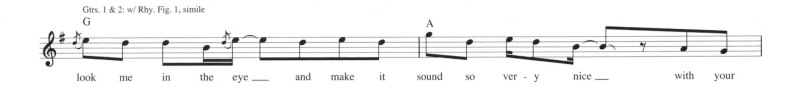

look me in the eye ___ and make it sound so ver-y nice ___ with your

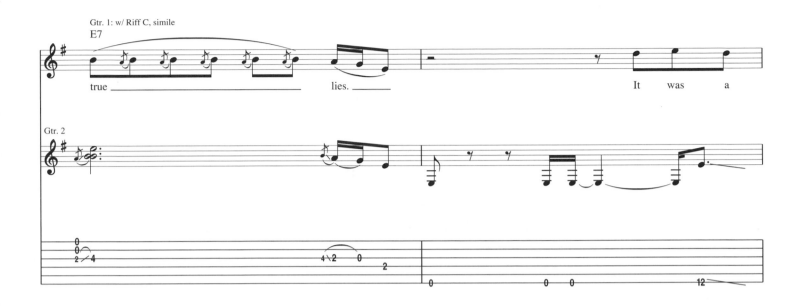

true ___ lies. It was a

clev-er dis-guise ___ but, girl, I'm get-tin' wise ___ to your

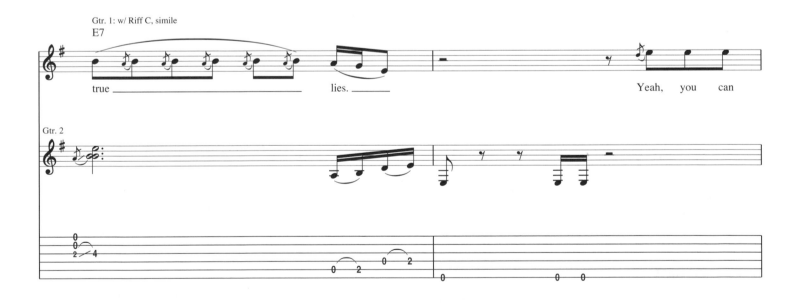

true ___ lies. ___ Yeah, you can

laugh, you can cry ___ but, girl, ___ I just can't buy ___ your

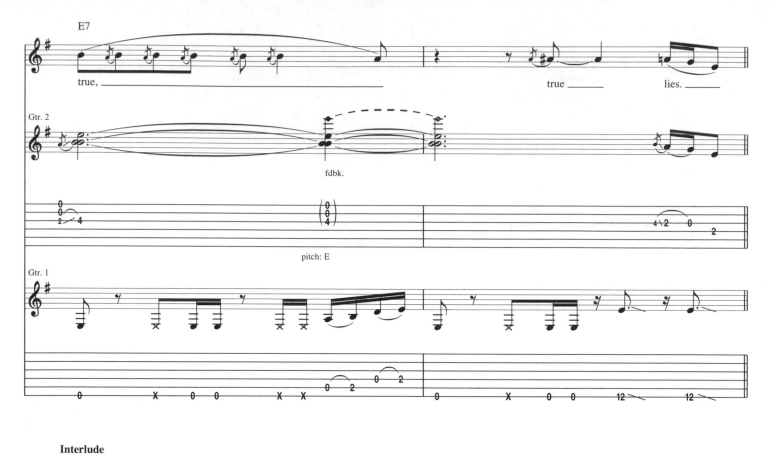

Interlude

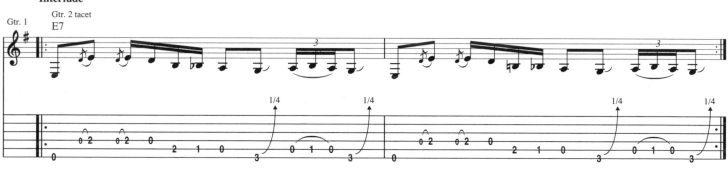

Guitar Solo

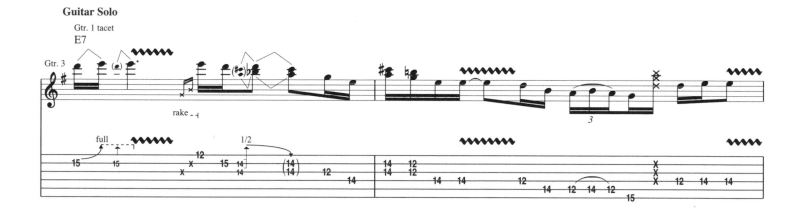

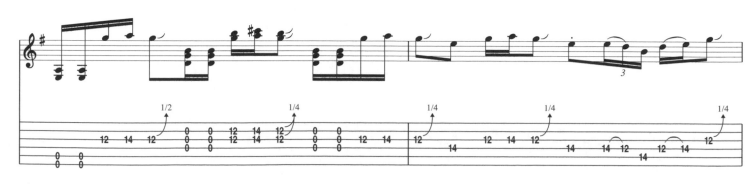

Twice as Hard

Words and Music by Chris Robinson and Rich Robinson

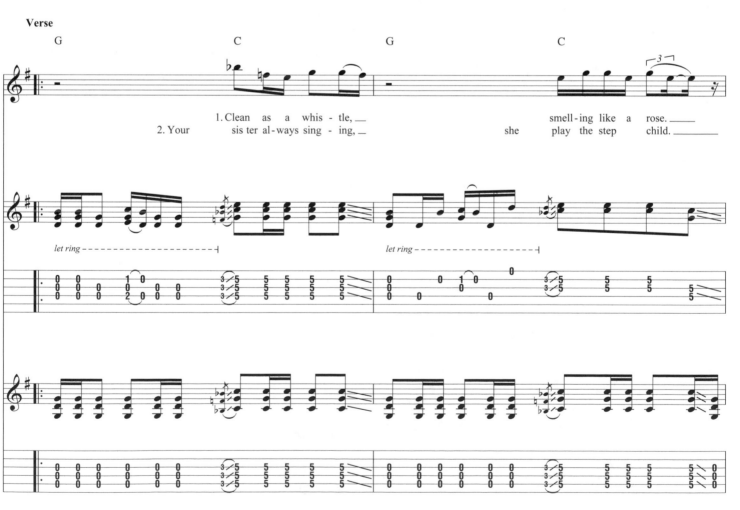

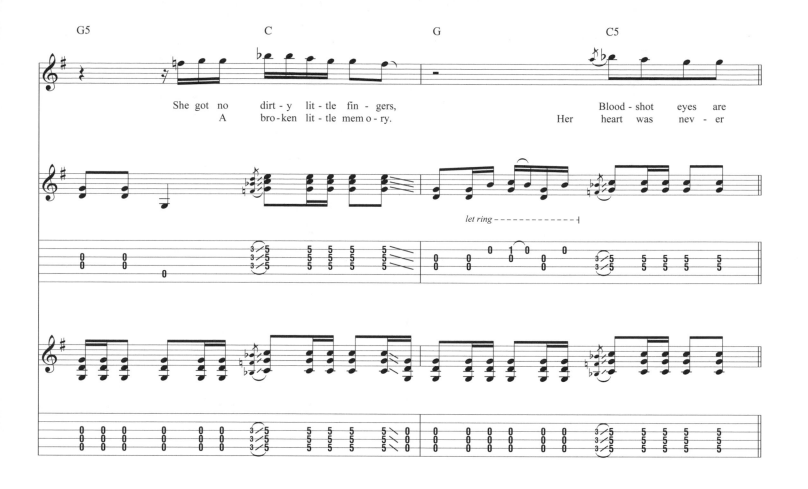

She got no   dirt - y   lit - tle   fin - gers,
A   bro - ken   lit - tle   mem - o - ry.
Blood - shot   eyes   are
Her   heart   was   nev - er

𝄋 **Pre-Chorus**

3rd time, Gtr. 3: w/ Fill 1

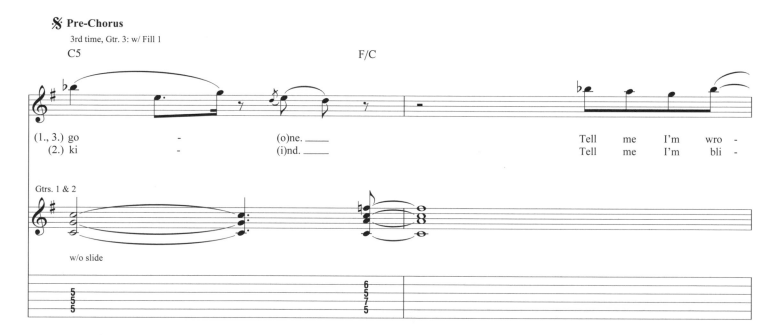

(1., 3.) go - (o)ne. _____
(2.) ki - (i)nd. _____
Tell   me   I'm   wro -
Tell   me   I'm   bli -

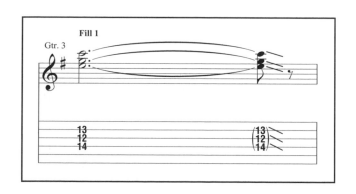

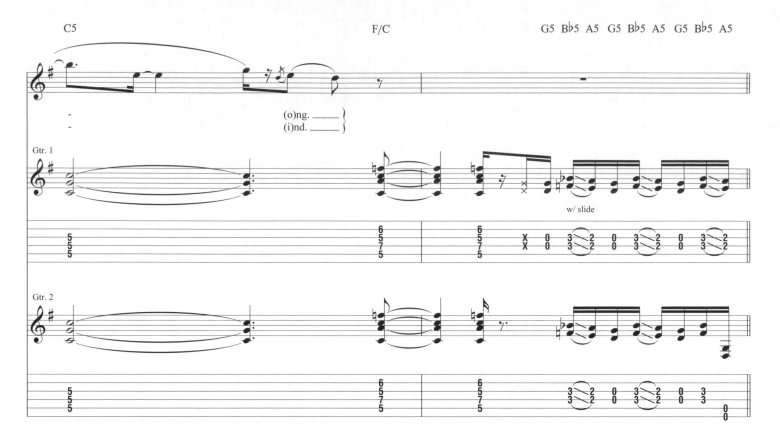

C5   F/C   G5 Bb5 A5 G5 Bb5 A5 G5 Bb5 A5

Gtr. 1

w/ slide

Gtr. 2

Chorus

1st time, Gtrs. 1 & 2: w/ Rhy. Fig. 1
2nd time, Gtrs. 1 & 2: w/ Rhy. Fill 1 (3 1/2 times)
3rd time, Rhy. Fill 1 & 2: w/ Rhy. Fill 1 (7 1/2 times)

G   C5   G   C5

Twice _____ as ha, hard __ as it was the first time __ I said good - bye. __

G   C5

_____ Twice _____ as ha, hard __ as it was the

To Coda ⊕

2nd time, Gtrs. 1 & 2: w/ Rhy. Fig. 1 (last 2 meas.)

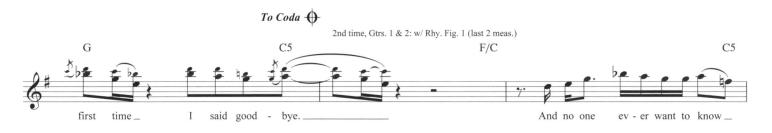

G   C5   F/C   C5

first time __ I said good - bye. _____ And no one ev - er want to know __

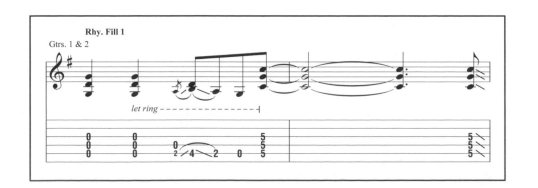

Rhy. Fill 1

Gtrs. 1 & 2

let ring - - - - - - - - - - - - - - - -

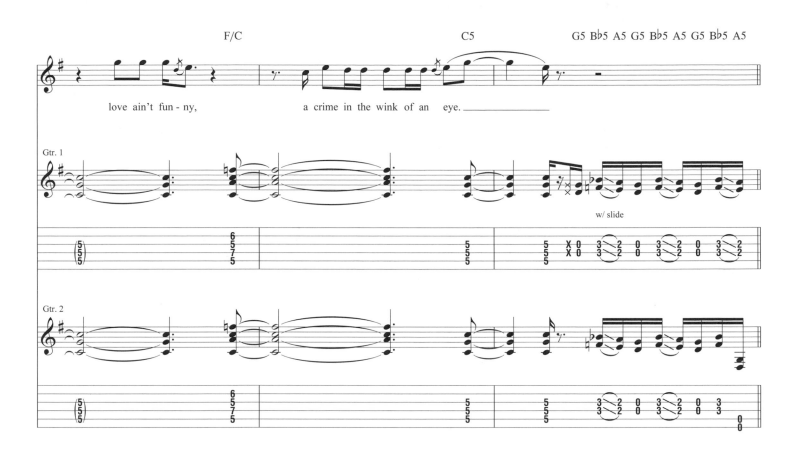

love ain't fun - ny,   a crime in the wink of an eye.

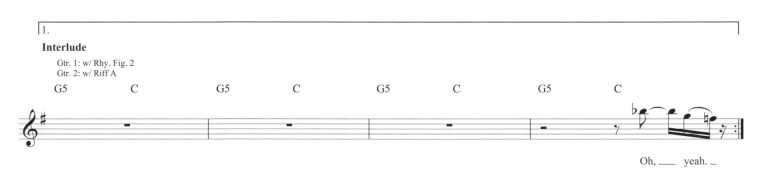

1.

Interlude

Gtr. 1: w/ Rhy. Fig. 2
Gtr. 2: w/ Riff A

G5   C   G5   C   G5   C   G5   C

Oh, ___ yeah. ___

2.

Guitar Solo

Gtr. 2 tacet

Gtr. 1: w/ Rhy. Fig. 3 (2 times)

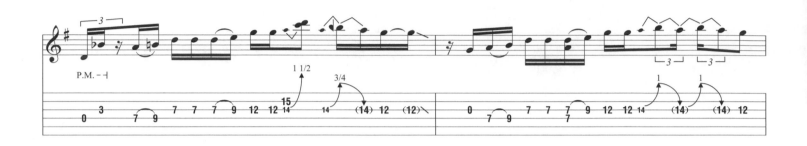

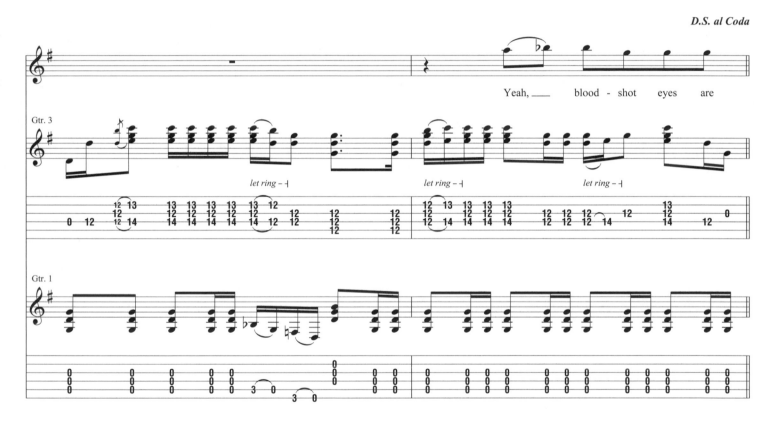

D.S. al Coda

Yeah, ___ blood - shot eyes are

Gtr. 3

let ring

Gtr. 1

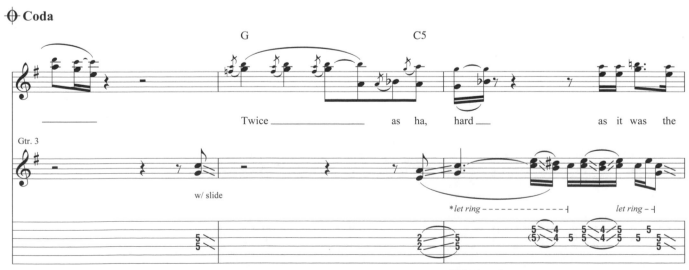

Coda

G   C5

Twice ___ as ha, hard ___ as it was the

Gtr. 3

w/ slide

let ring   *let ring*

*3rd string only.

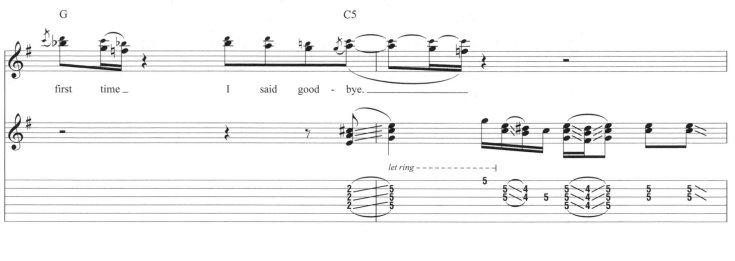

first time __   I said good - bye. _____

let ring - - - - - - - - - - - -

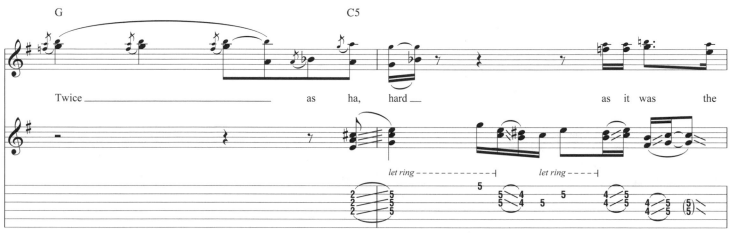

Twice _____ as ha, hard __   as it was the

let ring - - - - - - - - - - - -   *let ring - - - -*

Gtrs. 1 & 2: w/ Rhy. Fig. 1 (last 2 meas.)

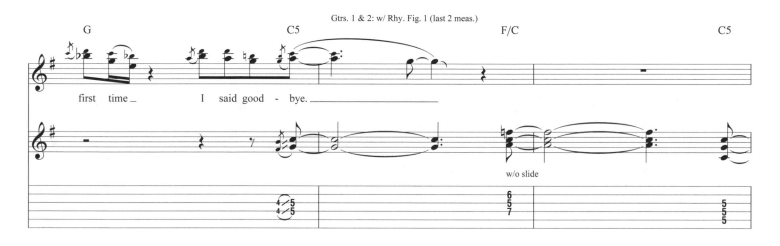

first time __   I said good - bye. _____

w/o slide

G5 B♭5 A5 G5 B♭5 A5 G5 B♭5 A5   G5 B♭5 A5 G5 B♭5 A5 G5   N.C.

Gtr. 3

w/ slide

*Gtrs. 1 & 2

w/ slide

*Composite arrangement

from Gary Moore - *Bad for You Baby*

Walking Through the Park

Written by Muddy Waters

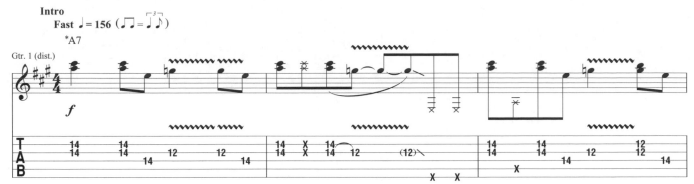

*Chord symbols reflect basic harmony.

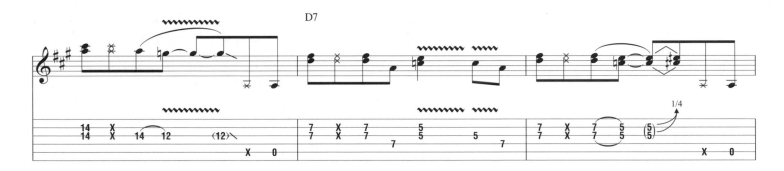

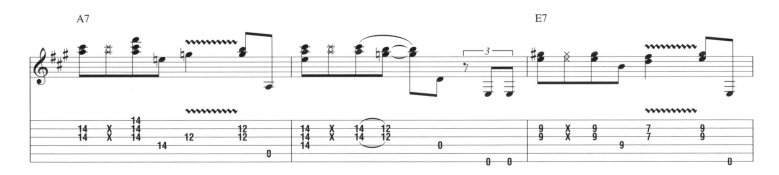

Verse

go - ing out walk - ing _____ 'long that old av - e - nue. _

Yes, I'm go - ing out walk - ing _____ 'long that old av - e -

nue. I'm __ gon - na walk for so long, _____

till she won't know __ what to do. Yeah!

Guitar Solo

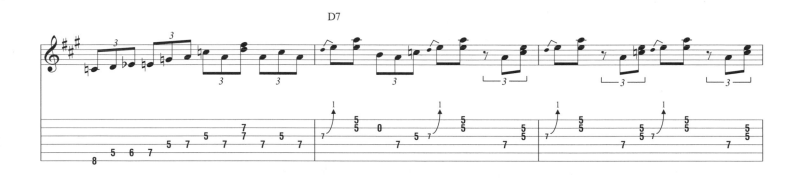

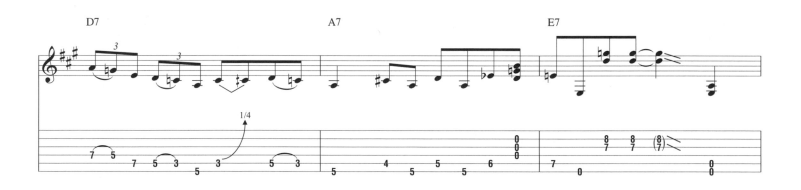

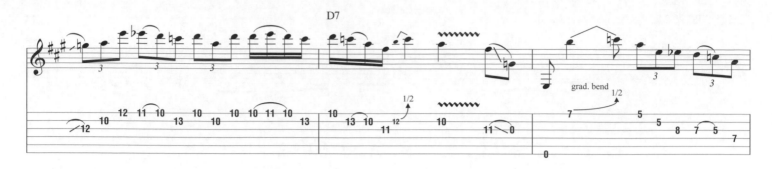

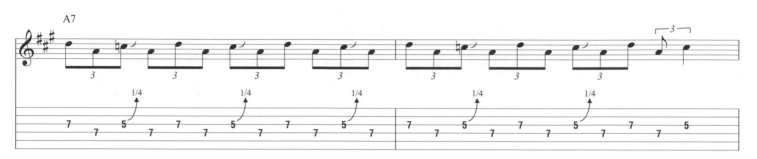

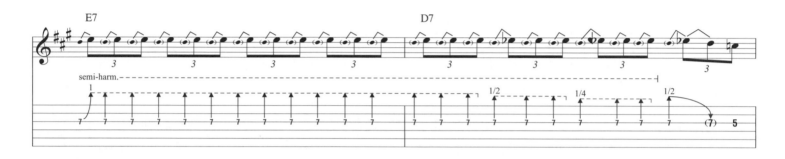

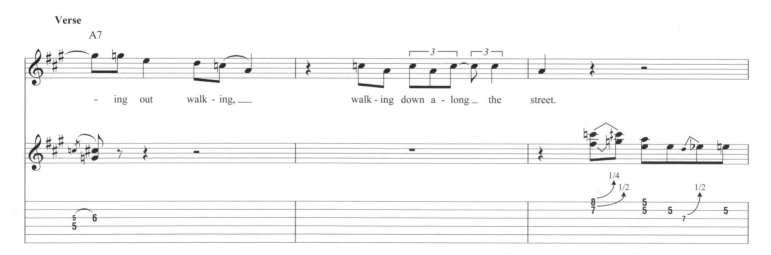

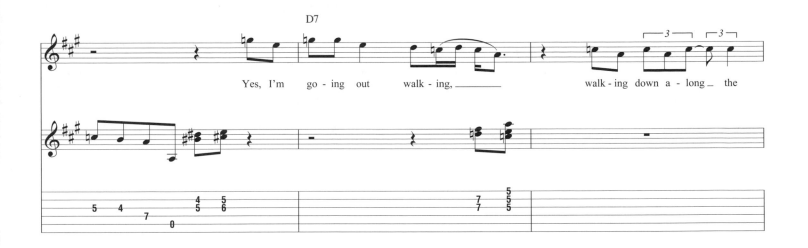

Yes, I'm go-ing out walk-ing, _____ walk-ing down a - long _ the

street. I'm ___ gon-na walk her be-side me,

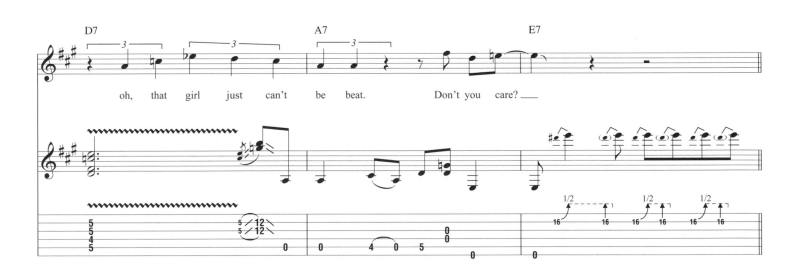

oh, that girl just can't be beat. Don't you care? ___

Guitar Solo

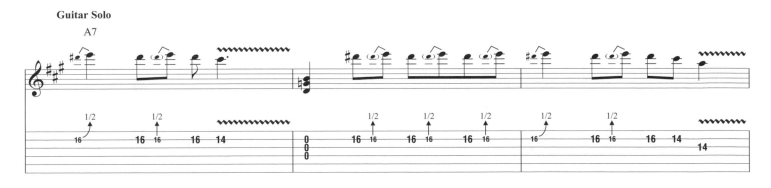

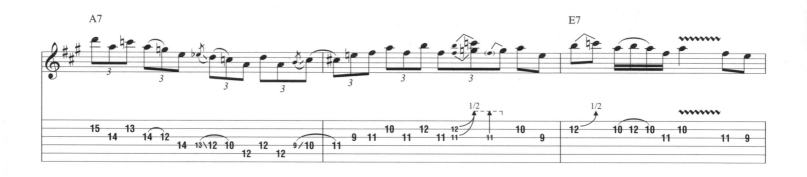

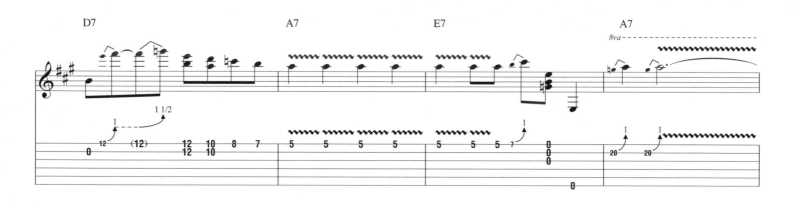

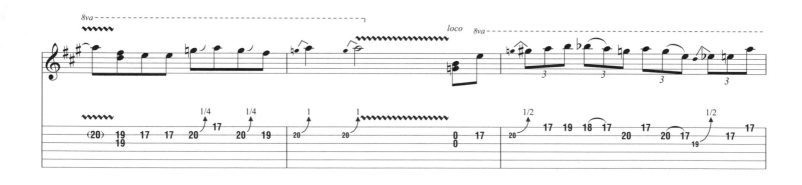

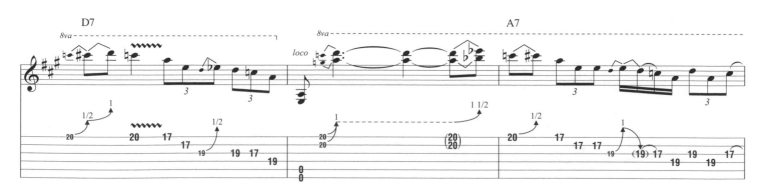

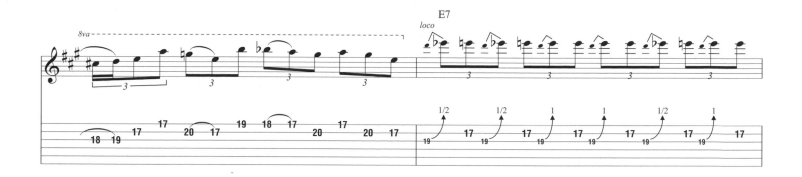

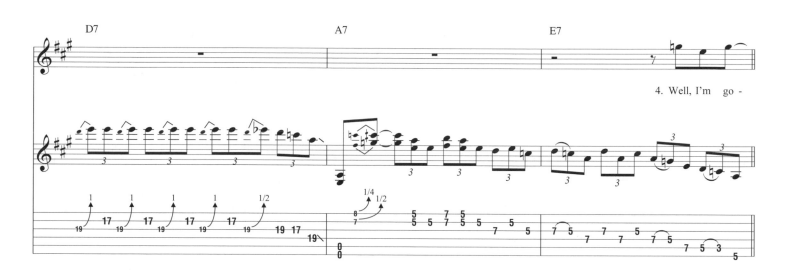

4. Well, I'm go-

Verse

-ing out walk-ing, ___ a, walk-ing down through the park.

Yes, I'm go-ing out walk-ing, ___ walk-ing down through the

park. ___   I'm ___ gon-na walk   in   the   moon - light

till   the   night   gets   dark.

Free time

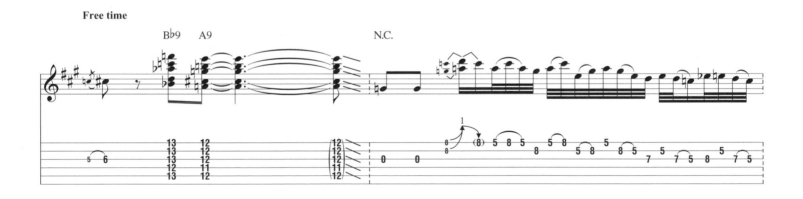

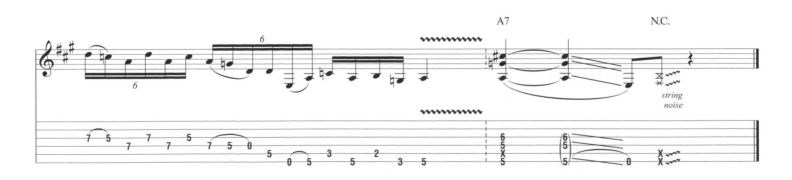

string
noise

GUITAR NOTATION LEGEND

Guitar music can be notated three different ways: on a *musical staff*, in *tablature*, and in *rhythm slashes*.

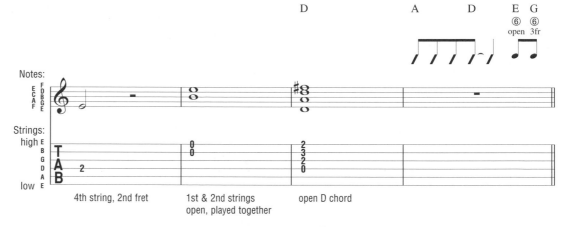

RHYTHM SLASHES are written above the staff. Strum chords in the rhythm indicated. Use the chord diagrams found at the top of the first page of the transcription for the appropriate chord voicings. Round noteheads indicate single notes.

THE MUSICAL STAFF shows pitches and rhythms and is divided by bar lines into measures. Pitches are named after the first seven letters of the alphabet.

TABLATURE graphically represents the guitar fingerboard. Each horizontal line represents a string, and each number represents a fret.

Notes:

Strings:
high E
B
G
D
A
low E

4th string, 2nd fret   1st & 2nd strings open, played together   open D chord

Definitions for Special Guitar Notation

HALF-STEP BEND: Strike the note and bend up 1/2 step.

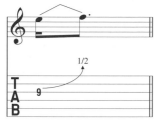

WHOLE-STEP BEND: Strike the note and bend up one step.

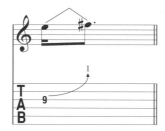

GRACE NOTE BEND: Strike the note and immediately bend up as indicated.

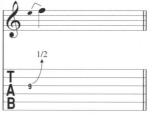

SLIGHT (MICROTONE) BEND: Strike the note and bend up 1/4 step.

BEND AND RELEASE: Strike the note and bend up as indicated, then release back to the original note. Only the first note is struck.

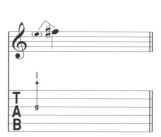

PRE-BEND: Bend the note as indicated, then strike it.

PRE-BEND AND RELEASE: Bend the note as indicated. Strike it and release the bend back to the original note.

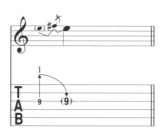

UNISON BEND: Strike the two notes simultaneously and bend the lower note up to the pitch of the higher.

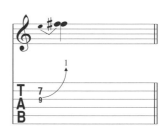

VIBRATO: The string is vibrated by rapidly bending and releasing the note with the fretting hand.

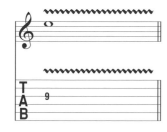

WIDE VIBRATO: The pitch is varied to a greater degree by vibrating with the fretting hand.

HAMMER-ON: Strike the first (lower) note with one finger, then sound the higher note (on the same string) with another finger by fretting it without picking.

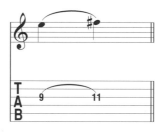

PULL-OFF: Place both fingers on the notes to be sounded. Strike the first note and without picking, pull the finger off to sound the second (lower) note.

LEGATO SLIDE: Strike the first note and then slide the same fret-hand finger up or down to the second note. The second note is not struck.

SHIFT SLIDE: Same as legato slide, except the second note is struck.

TRILL: Very rapidly alternate between the notes indicated by continuously hammering on and pulling off.

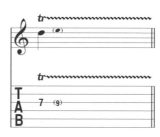

TAPPING: Hammer ("tap") the fret indicated with the pick-hand index or middle finger and pull off to the note fretted by the fret hand.

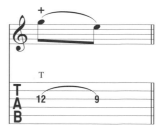

NATURAL HARMONIC: Strike the note while the fret-hand lightly touches the string directly over the fret indicated.

PINCH HARMONIC: The note is fretted normally and a harmonic is produced by adding the edge of the thumb or the tip of the index finger of the pick hand to the normal pick attack.

HARP HARMONIC: The note is fretted normally and a harmonic is produced by gently resting the pick hand's index finger directly above the indicated fret (in parentheses) while the pick hand's thumb or pick assists by plucking the appropriate string.

PICK SCRAPE: The edge of the pick is rubbed down (or up) the string, producing a scratchy sound.

MUFFLED STRINGS: A percussive sound is produced by laying the fret hand across the string(s) without depressing, and striking them with the pick hand.

PALM MUTING: The note is partially muted by the pick hand lightly touching the string(s) just before the bridge.

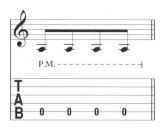

RAKE: Drag the pick across the strings indicated with a single motion.

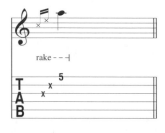

TREMOLO PICKING: The note is picked as rapidly and continuously as possible.

ARPEGGIATE: Play the notes of the chord indicated by quickly rolling them from bottom to top.

VIBRATO BAR DIVE AND RETURN: The pitch of the note or chord is dropped a specified number of steps (in rhythm), then returned to the original pitch.

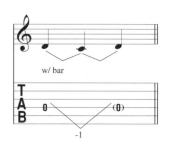

VIBRATO BAR SCOOP: Depress the bar just before striking the note, then quickly release the bar.

VIBRATO BAR DIP: Strike the note and then immediately drop a specified number of steps, then release back to the original pitch.

Additional Musical Definitions

 (accent) • Accentuate note (play it louder).

 (accent) • Accentuate note with great intensity.

 (staccato) • Play the note short.

 • Downstroke

V • Upstroke

D.S. al Coda • Go back to the sign (𝄋), then play until the measure marked "*To Coda*," then skip to the section labelled "**Coda**."

D.C. al Fine • Go back to the beginning of the song and play until the measure marked "*Fine*" (end).

Rhy. Fig. • Label used to recall a recurring accompaniment pattern (usually chordal).

Riff • Label used to recall composed, melodic lines (usually single notes) which recur.

Fill • Label used to identify a brief melodic figure which is to be inserted into the arrangement.

Rhy. Fill • A chordal version of a Fill.

tacet • Instrument is silent (drops out).

 • Repeat measures between signs.

 • When a repeated section has different endings, play the first ending only the first time and the second ending only the second time.

NOTE: Tablature numbers in parentheses mean:
   1. The note is being sustained over a system (note in standard notation is tied), or
   2. The note is sustained, but a new articulation (such as a hammer-on, pull-off, slide or vibrato) begins, or
   3. The note is a barely audible "ghost" note (note in standard notation is also in parentheses).

TAB+

Accurate Tabs
Gear Information
Selected Pedal Settings
Analysis & Playing Tips

The Tab+ Series gives you note-for-note accurate transcriptions in notes and tab PLUS a whole lot more. These books also include performance notes to help you master the song, tips on the essential gear to make the song sound its best, recording techniques, historical information, right- and left-hand techniques and other playing tips – it's all here!

TAB. TONE. TECHNIQUE.

25 TOP ACOUSTIC SONGS

Big Yellow Taxi • Can't Find My Way Home • Cat's in the Cradle • The Clap • Closer to the Heart • Free Fallin' • Going to California • Good Riddance (Time of Your Life) • Hey There Delilah • A Horse with No Name • I Got a Name • Into the Mystic • Lola • Losing My Religion • Love the One You're With • Never Going Back Again • Norwegian Wood (This Bird Has Flown) • Ooh La La • Patience • She Talks to Angels • Shower the People • Tequila Sunrise • The Weight • Wild Horses • Wish You Were Here.
00109283 .... $19.99

25 TOP CLASSIC ROCK SONGS

Addicted to Love • After Midnight • Another Brick in the Wall, Part 2 • Aqualung • Beat It • Brown Sugar • China Grove • Domino • Dream On • For What It's Worth • Fortunate Son • Go Your Own Way • Had to Cry Today • Keep Your Hands to Yourself • Life in the Fast Lane • Lights • Message in a Bottle • Peace of Mind • Reeling in the Years • Refugee • Rock and Roll Never Forgets • Roundabout • Tom Sawyer • Up on Cripple Creek • Wild Night.
00102519 .... $19.99

25 TOP HARD ROCK SONGS

Back in Black • Best of Both Worlds • Crazy Train • Detroit Rock City • Doctor, Doctor • Fire Woman • Hair of the Dog • In My Dreams • In-A-Gadda-Da-Vida • Jailbreak • Nobody's Fool • Paranoid • Rock Candy • Rock of Ages • School's Out • Shout at the Devil • Smoke on the Water • Still of the Night • Stone Cold • Welcome to the Jungle • Whole Lotta Love • Working Man • You've Got Another Thing Comin' • Youth Gone Wild • The Zoo.
00102469 .... $19.99

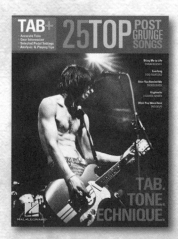

25 TOP METAL SONGS

Ace of Spades • Afterlife • Am I Evil? • Blackout • Breaking the Law • Chop Suey! • Cowboys from Hell • Down with the Sickness • Evil • Freak on a Leash • Hangar 18 • Iron Man • Laid to Rest • The Last in Line • Madhouse • Mr. Crowley • Psychosocial • Pull Me Under • Raining Blood • Roots Bloody Roots • Sober • Tears Don't Fall • Thunder Kiss '65 • The Trooper • Unsung.
00102501 .... $19.99

25 TOP POST-GRUNGE SONGS

All Star • Bawitdaba • Blurry • Boulevard of Broken Dreams • Bring Me to Life • Closing Time • Devour • Du Hast • Everlong • Far Behind • Hero • How You Remind Me • I Hate Everything About You • I Stand Alone • It's Been Awhile • Kryptonite • Metalingus • My Own Summer (Shove It) • One Last Breath • One Week • The Reason • Remedy • Sex and Candy • Thnks Fr Th Mmrs • Wish You Were Here.
00102518 .... $19.99

HAL•LEONARD®
CORPORATION
7777 W. BLUEMOUND RD. P.O. BOX 13819
MILWAUKEE, WISCONSIN 53213

www.halleonard.com

Prices, contents, and availability subject to change without notice.

GUITAR RECORDED VERSIONS®

Guitar Recorded Versions® are note-for-note transcriptions of guitar music taken directly off recordings. This series, one of the most popular in print today, features some of the greatest guitar players and groups from blues and rock to country and jazz.

Guitar Recorded Versions are transcribed by the best transcribers in the business. Every book contains notes and tablature. Visit **www.halleonard.com** for our complete selection.

AUTHENTIC TRANSCRIPTIONS
WITH NOTES AND TABLATURE

00690169 Eric Johnson – Venus Isle $22.95
00122439 Jack Johnson – From Here to Now to You $22.99
00690846 Jack Johnson and Friends – Sing-A-Longs and Lullabies for the Film Curious George $19.95
00690271 Robert Johnson – The New Transcriptions $24.95
00699131 Best of Janis Joplin $19.95
00690427 Best of Judas Priest $22.99
00690277 Best of Kansas $19.95
00690911 Best of Phil Keaggy $24.99
00690727 Toby Keith Guitar Collection $19.99
00120814 Killswitch Engage – Disarm the Descent $22.99
00690504 Very Best of Albert King $19.95
00690444 B.B. King & Eric Clapton – Riding with the King $22.99
00690134 Freddie King Collection $19.95
00691062 Kings of Leon – Come Around Sundown $22.99
00690157 Kiss – Alive! $19.95
00690356 Kiss – Alive II $22.99
00694903 Best of Kiss for Guitar $24.95
00690355 Kiss – Destroyer $16.95
14026320 Mark Knopfler – Get Lucky $22.99
00690164 Mark Knopfler Guitar – Vol. 1 $19.95
00690163 Mark Knopfler/Chet Atkins – Neck and Neck $19.95
00690780 Korn – Greatest Hits, Volume 1 $22.95
00690377 Kris Kristofferson Collection $19.95
00690834 Lamb of God – Ashes of the Wake $19.95
00690875 Lamb of God – Sacrament $19.95
00690977 Ray LaMontagne – Gossip in the Grain $19.99
00690823 Ray LaMontagne – Trouble $19.95
00691057 Ray LaMontagne and the Pariah Dogs – God Willin' & The Creek Don't Rise $22.99
00690781 Linkin Park – Hybrid Theory $22.95
00690782 Linkin Park – Meteora $22.95
00690922 Linkin Park – Minutes to Midnight $19.95
00699623 The Best of Chuck Loeb $19.95
00114563 The Lumineers $22.99
00690525 Best of George Lynch $24.99
00690955 Lynyrd Skynyrd – All-Time Greatest Hits $19.99
00694954 New Best of Lynyrd Skynyrd $19.95
00690577 Yngwie Malmsteen – Anthology $24.95
00690754 Marilyn Manson – Lest We Forget $19.95
00694956 Bob Marley – Legend $19.95
00690548 Very Best of Bob Marley & The Wailers – One Love $22.99
00694945 Bob Marley – Songs of Freedom $24.95
00690914 Maroon 5 – It Won't Be Soon Before Long $19.95
00690657 Maroon 5 – Songs About Jane $19.95
00690748 Maroon 5 – 1.22.03 Acoustic $19.95
00690989 Mastodon – Crack the Skye $22.99
00119220 Brent Mason – Hot Wired $19.99
00691176 Mastodon – The Hunter $22.99
00690616 Matchbox Twenty – More Than You Think You Are $19.95
00690239 Matchbox 20 – Yourself or Someone like You $19.95
00691942 Andy McKee – Art of Motion $22.99
00691034 Andy McKee – Joyland $19.99
00690382 Sarah McLachlan – Mirrorball $19.95
00120080 The Don McLean Songbook $19.95
00694952 Megadeth – Countdown to Extinction $22.95
00690244 Megadeth – Cryptic Writings $19.95
00694951 Megadeth – Rust in Peace $22.95
00690011 Megadeth – Youthanasia $19.95
00690505 John Mellencamp Guitar Collection $19.95
00690562 Pat Metheny – Bright Size Life $19.95
00691073 Pat Metheny with Christian McBride & Antonion Sanchez – Day Trip/Tokyo Day Trip Live $22.99
00690646 Pat Metheny – One Quiet Night $19.95
00690559 Pat Metheny – Question & Answer $19.95
00118836 Pat Metheny – Unity Band $22.99
00102590 Pat Metheny – What's It All About $22.99
00690040 Steve Miller Band Greatest Hits $19.95
00119338 Ministry Guitar Tab Collection $24.99
00690769 Modest Mouse – Good News for People Who Love Bad News $19.95
00102591 Wes Montgomery Guitar Anthology $24.99
00694802 Gary Moore – Still Got the Blues $22.99
00691005 Best of Motion City Soundtrack $19.99
00690787 Mudvayne – L.D. 50 $22.95
00691070 Mumford & Sons – Sigh No More $22.99
00118196 Muse – The 2nd Law $19.99
00690996 My Morning Jacket Collection $19.99
00690984 Matt Nathanson – Some Mad Hope $22.99
00690611 Nirvana $22.95
00694895 Nirvana – Bleach $19.95
00694913 Nirvana – In Utero $19.95
00694883 Nirvana – Nevermind $19.95
00690026 Nirvana – Unplugged in New York $19.95
00120112 No Doubt – Tragic Kingdom $22.95
00690226 Oasis – The Other Side of Oasis $19.95
00307163 Oasis – Time Flies... 1994-2009 $19.99
00690818 The Best of Opeth $22.95
00691052 Roy Orbison – Black & White Night $22.99
00694847 Best of Ozzy Osbourne $22.95
00690399 Ozzy Osbourne – The Ozzman Cometh $22.99
00690129 Ozzy Osbourne – Ozzmosis $22.95
00690933 Best of Brad Paisley $22.95
00690995 Brad Paisley – Play: The Guitar Album $24.99
00690939 Christopher Parkening – Solo Pieces $19.99
00690594 Best of Les Paul $19.95
00694855 Pearl Jam – Ten $22.99
00690439 A Perfect Circle – Mer De Noms $19.95
00690725 Best of Carl Perkins $19.99
00690499 Tom Petty – Definitive Guitar Collection $19.95
00690868 Tom Petty – Highway Companion $19.95
00690176 Phish – Billy Breathes $22.95
00691249 Phish – Junta $22.99
00690428 Pink Floyd – Dark Side of the Moon $19.95
00690789 Best of Poison $19.95
00690299 Best of Elvis: The King of Rock 'n' Roll $19.95
00692535 Elvis Presley $19.95
00690925 The Very Best of Prince $22.99
00690003 Classic Queen $24.95
00694975 Queen – Greatest Hits $24.95
00690670 Very Best of Queensryche $19.95
00690878 The Raconteurs – Broken Boy Soldiers $19.95
00109303 Radiohead Guitar Anthology $24.99
00694910 Rage Against the Machine $19.95
00119834 Rage Against the Machine – Guitar Anthology $22.99
00690179 Rancid – And Out Come the Wolves $22.95
00690426 Best of Ratt $19.95
00690055 Red Hot Chili Peppers – Blood Sugar Sex Magik $19.95
00690584 Red Hot Chili Peppers – By the Way $19.95
00690379 Red Hot Chili Peppers – Californication $19.95
00690673 Red Hot Chili Peppers – Greatest Hits $19.95
00690090 Red Hot Chili Peppers – One Hot Minute $22.95
00691166 Red Hot Chili Peppers – I'm with You $22.99
00690852 Red Hot Chili Peppers – Stadium Arcadium $24.95
00690511 Django Reinhardt – The Definitive Collection $19.95
00690779 Relient K – MMHMM $19.95
00690643 Relient K – Two Lefts Don't Make a Right ... But Three Do $19.95
00690260 Jimmie Rodgers Guitar Collection $19.95
14041901 Rodrigo Y Gabriela and C.U.B.A. – Area 52 $24.99
00690014 Rolling Stones – Exile on Main Street $24.95
00690631 Rolling Stones – Guitar Anthology $27.95
00690685 David Lee Roth – Eat 'Em and Smile $19.95
00690031 Santana's Greatest Hits $19.95
00690796 Very Best of Michael Schenker $19.95
00690566 Best of Scorpions $22.95
00690604 Bob Seger – Guitar Anthology $19.95
00691012 Shadows Fall – Retribution $22.99
00690803 Best of Kenny Wayne Shepherd Band $19.95
00690750 Kenny Wayne Shepherd – The Place You're In $19.95
00690857 Shinedown – Us and Them $19.95
00122218 Skillet – Rise $22.99
00690872 Slayer – Christ Illusion $19.95
00690813 Slayer – Guitar Collection $19.95
00690419 Slipknot $19.95
00690973 Slipknot – All Hope Is Gone $22.99
00690330 Social Distortion – Live at the Roxy $19.95
00120004 Best of Steely Dan $24.95
00694921 Best of Steppenwolf $22.95
00690655 Best of Mike Stern $19.95
14041588 Cat Stevens – Tea for the Tillerman $19.99
00690949 Rod Stewart Guitar Anthology $19.99
00690021 Sting – Fields of Gold $19.95
00690520 Styx Guitar Collection $19.95
00120081 Sublime $19.95
00690992 Sublime – Robbin' the Hood $19.99
00690519 SUM 41 – All Killer No Filler $19.95
00691072 Best of Supertramp $22.99
00690994 Taylor Swift $22.99
00690993 Taylor Swift – Fearless $22.99
00115957 Taylor Swift – Red $21.99
00691063 Taylor Swift – Speak Now $22.99
00690767 Switchfoot – The Beautiful Letdown $19.95
00690531 System of a Down – Toxicity $19.95

RECORDED VERSIONS GUITAR®

AUTHENTIC TRANSCRIPTIONS WITH NOTES AND TABLATURE

00694824 Best of James Taylor $17.99
00694887 Best of Thin Lizzy $19.95
00690871 Three Days Grace – One-X $19.95
00690891 30 Seconds to Mars – A Beautiful Lie $19.95
00690233 The Merle Travis Collection $19.99
00690683 Robin Trower – Bridge of Sighs $19.95
00699191 U2 – Best of: 1980-1990 $19.95
00690732 U2 – Best of: 1990-2000 $19.95
00690894 U2 – 18 Singles $19.95
00690039 Steve Vai – Alien Love Secrets $24.95
00690172 Steve Vai – Fire Garden $24.95
00660137 Steve Vai – Passion & Warfare $24.95
00690881 Steve Vai – Real Illusions: Reflections $24.95
00694904 Steve Vai – Sex and Religion $24.95
00110385 Steve Vai – The Story of Light $22.99
00690392 Steve Vai – The Ultra Zone $19.95
00700555 Van Halen – Van Halen $19.99
00690024 Stevie Ray Vaughan – Couldn't Stand the Weather $19.95
00690370 Stevie Ray Vaughan and Double Trouble – The Real Deal: Greatest Hits Volume 2 $22.95
00690116 Stevie Ray Vaughan – Guitar Collection $24.95
00660136 Stevie Ray Vaughan – In Step $19.95
00694879 Stevie Ray Vaughan – In the Beginning $19.95
00660058 Stevie Ray Vaughan – Lightnin' Blues '83-'87 $24.95
00690036 Stevie Ray Vaughan – Live Alive $24.95
00694835 Stevie Ray Vaughan – The Sky Is Crying $22.95
00690025 Stevie Ray Vaughan – Soul to Soul $19.95
00690015 Stevie Ray Vaughan – Texas Flood $19.95
00690772 Velvet Revolver – Contraband $22.95
00109770 Volbeat Guitar Collection $22.99
00121808 Volbeat – Outlaw Gentlemen & Shady Ladies $22.99
00690132 The T-Bone Walker Collection $19.95
00694789 Muddy Waters – Deep Blues $24.95
00690071 Weezer (The Blue Album) $19.95
00690516 Weezer (The Green Album) $19.95
00690286 Weezer – Pinkerton $19.95
00691046 Weezer – Rarities Edition $22.99
00117511 Whitesnake Guitar Collection $19.99
00690447 Best of the Who $24.95
00691941 The Who – Acoustic Guitar Collection $22.99
00691006 Wilco Guitar Collection $22.99
00690672 Best of Dar Williams $19.95
00691017 Wolfmother – Cosmic Egg $22.99
00690319 Stevie Wonder – Some of the Best $17.95
00690596 Best of the Yardbirds $19.95
00690844 Yellowcard – Lights and Sounds $19.95
00690916 The Best of Dwight Yoakam $19.95
00691020 Neil Young – After the Goldrush $22.99
00691019 Neil Young – Everybody Knows This Is Nowhere $19.99
00690904 Neil Young – Harvest $29.99
00691021 Neil Young – Harvest Moon $22.99
00690905 Neil Young – Rust Never Sleeps $19.99
00690443 Frank Zappa – Hot Rats $19.95
00690624 Frank Zappa and the Mothers of Invention – One Size Fits All $22.99
00690623 Frank Zappa – Over-Nite Sensation $22.99
00121684 ZZ Top – Early Classics $24.99
00690589 ZZ Top – Guitar Anthology $24.95
00690960 ZZ Top Guitar Classics $19.99

HAL•LEONARD® CORPORATION
7777 W. Bluemound Rd. P.O. Box 13819 Milwaukee, WI 53213

Complete songlists and more at **www.halleonard.com**

Prices, contents, and availability subject to change without notice.

0314

HAL•LEONARD GUITAR PLAY•ALONG

This series will help you play your favorite songs quickly and easily. Just follow the tab and listen to the CD to the hear how the guitar should sound, and then play along using the separate backing tracks. Mac or PC users can also slow down the tempo without changing pitch by using the CD in their computer. The melody and lyrics are included in the book so that you can sing or simply follow along.

INCLUDES TAB

VOL. 1 – ROCK	00699570 / $16.99
VOL. 2 – ACOUSTIC	00699569 / $16.95
VOL. 3 – HARD ROCK	00699573 / $16.95
VOL. 4 – POP/ROCK	00699571 / $16.99
VOL. 5 – MODERN ROCK	00699574 / $16.99
VOL. 6 – '90S ROCK	00699572 / $16.99
VOL. 7 – BLUES	00699575 / $16.95
VOL. 8 – ROCK	00699585 / $14.99
VOL. 9 – PUNK ROCK	00699576 / $14.95
VOL. 10 – ACOUSTIC	00699586 / $16.95
VOL. 11 – EARLY ROCK	00699579 / $14.95
VOL. 12 – POP/ROCK	00699587 / $14.95
VOL. 13 – FOLK ROCK	00699581 / $15.99
VOL. 14 – BLUES ROCK	00699582 / $16.95
VOL. 15 – R&B	00699583 / $14.95
VOL. 16 – JAZZ	00699584 / $15.95
VOL. 17 – COUNTRY	00699588 / $15.95
VOL. 18 – ACOUSTIC ROCK	00699577 / $15.95
VOL. 19 – SOUL	00699578 / $14.99
VOL. 20 – ROCKABILLY	00699580 / $14.95
VOL. 21 – YULETIDE	00699602 / $14.95
VOL. 22 – CHRISTMAS	00699600 / $15.95
VOL. 23 – SURF	00699635 / $14.95
VOL. 24 – ERIC CLAPTON	00699649 / $17.99
VOL. 25 – LENNON & MCCARTNEY	00699642 / $16.99
VOL. 26 – ELVIS PRESLEY	00699643 / $14.95
VOL. 27 – DAVID LEE ROTH	00699645 / $16.95
VOL. 28 – GREG KOCH	00699646 / $14.95
VOL. 29 – BOB SEGER	00699647 / $15.99
VOL. 30 – KISS	00699644 / $16.99
VOL. 31 – CHRISTMAS HITS	00699652 / $14.95
VOL. 32 – THE OFFSPRING	00699653 / $14.95
VOL. 33 – ACOUSTIC CLASSICS	00699656 / $16.95
VOL. 34 – CLASSIC ROCK	00699658 / $16.95
VOL. 35 – HAIR METAL	00699660 / $16.95
VOL. 36 – SOUTHERN ROCK	00699661 / $16.95
VOL. 37 – ACOUSTIC UNPLUGGED	00699662 / $16.99
VOL. 38 – BLUES	00699663 / $16.95
VOL. 39 – '80S METAL	00699664 / $16.99
VOL. 40 – INCUBUS	00699668 / $17.95
VOL. 41 – ERIC CLAPTON	00699669 / $16.95
VOL. 42 – 2000S ROCK	00699670 / $16.99
VOL. 43 – LYNYRD SKYNYRD	00699681 / $17.95
VOL. 44 – JAZZ	00699689 / $14.99
VOL. 45 – TV THEMES	00699718 / $14.95
VOL. 46 – MAINSTREAM ROCK	00699722 / $16.95
VOL. 47 – HENDRIX SMASH HITS	00699723 / $19.95
VOL. 48 – AEROSMITH CLASSICS	00699724 / $17.99
VOL. 49 – STEVIE RAY VAUGHAN	00699725 / $17.99
VOL. 51 – ALTERNATIVE '90S	00699727 / $14.99
VOL. 52 – FUNK	00699728 / $14.95
VOL. 53 – DISCO	00699729 / $14.99
VOL. 54 – HEAVY METAL	00699730 / $14.95
VOL. 55 – POP METAL	00699731 / $14.95

VOL. 56 – FOO FIGHTERS	00699749 / $15.99
VOL. 57 – SYSTEM OF A DOWN	00699751 / $14.95
VOL. 58 – BLINK-182	00699772 / $14.95
VOL. 59 – CHET ATKINS	00702347 / $16.99
VOL. 60 – 3 DOORS DOWN	00699774 / $14.95
VOL. 61 – SLIPKNOT	00699775 / $16.99
VOL. 62 – CHRISTMAS CAROLS	00699798 / $12.95
VOL. 63 – CREEDENCE CLEARWATER REVIVAL	00699802 / $16.99
VOL. 64 – THE ULTIMATE OZZY OSBOURNE	00699803 / $16.99
VOL. 66 – THE ROLLING STONES	00699807 / $16.95
VOL. 67 – BLACK SABBATH	00699808 / $16.99
VOL. 68 – PINK FLOYD – DARK SIDE OF THE MOON	00699809 / $16.99
VOL. 69 – ACOUSTIC FAVORITES	00699810 / $14.95
VOL. 70 – OZZY OSBOURNE	00699805 / $16.99
VOL. 71 – CHRISTIAN ROCK	00699824 / $14.95
VOL. 73 – BLUESY ROCK	00699829 / $16.99
VOL. 75 – TOM PETTY	00699882 / $16.99
VOL. 76 – COUNTRY HITS	00699884 / $14.95
VOL. 77 – BLUEGRASS	00699910 / $14.99
VOL. 78 – NIRVANA	00700132 / $16.99
VOL. 79 – NEIL YOUNG	00700133 / $24.99
VOL. 80 – ACOUSTIC ANTHOLOGY	00700175 / $19.95
VOL. 81 – ROCK ANTHOLOGY	00700176 / $22.99
VOL. 82 – EASY SONGS	00700177 / $12.99
VOL. 83 – THREE CHORD SONGS	00700178 / $16.99
VOL. 84 – STEELY DAN	00700200 / $16.99
VOL. 85 – THE POLICE	00700269 /$16.99
VOL. 86 – BOSTON	00700465 / $16.99
VOL. 87 – ACOUSTIC WOMEN	00700763 / $14.99
VOL. 88 – GRUNGE	00700467 / $16.99
VOL. 89 – REGGAE	00700468 / $15.99
VOL. 90 – CLASSICAL POP	00700469 / $14.99
VOL. 91 – BLUES INSTRUMENTALS	00700505 / $14.99
VOL. 92 – EARLY ROCK INSTRUMENTALS	00700506 / $14.99
VOL. 93 – ROCK INSTRUMENTALS	00700507 / $16.99
VOL. 95 – BLUES CLASSICS	00700509 / $14.99
VOL. 96 – THIRD DAY	00700560 / $14.95
VOL. 97 – ROCK BAND	00700703 / $14.99
VOL. 99 – ZZ TOP	00700762 / $16.99
VOL. 100 – B.B. KING	00700466 / $16.99
VOL. 101 – SONGS FOR BEGINNERS	00701917 / $14.99
VOL. 102 – CLASSIC PUNK	00700769 / $14.99
VOL. 103 – SWITCHFOOT	00700773 / $16.99
VOL. 104 – DUANE ALLMAN	00700846 / $16.99
VOL. 106 – WEEZER	00700958 / $14.99
VOL. 107 – CREAM	00701069 / $16.99
VOL. 108 – THE WHO	00701053 / $16.99
VOL. 109 – STEVE MILLER	00701054 / $14.99
VOL. 111 – JOHN MELLENCAMP	00701056 / $14.99
VOL. 112 – QUEEN	00701052 / $16.99

VOL. 113 – JIM CROCE	00701058 / $15.99
VOL. 114 – BON JOVI	00701060 / $14.99
VOL. 115 – JOHNNY CASH	00701070 / $16.99
VOL. 116 – THE VENTURES	00701124 / $14.99
VOL. 117 – BRAD PAISLEY	00701224/ $16.99
VOL. 118 – ERIC JOHNSON	00701353 / $16.99
VOL. 119 – AC/DC CLASSICS	00701356 / $17.99
VOL. 120 – PROGRESSIVE ROCK	00701457 / $14.99
VOL. 121 – U2	00701508 / $16.99
VOL. 123 – LENNON & MCCARTNEY ACOUSTIC	00701614 / $16.99
VOL. 124 – MODERN WORSHIP	00701629 / $14.99
VOL. 125 – JEFF BECK	00701687 / $16.99
VOL. 126 – BOB MARLEY	00701701 / $16.99
VOL. 127 – 1970S ROCK	00701739 / $14.99
VOL. 128 – 1960S ROCK	00701740 / $14.99
VOL. 129 – MEGADETH	00701741 / $16.99
VOL. 131 – 1990S ROCK	00701743 / $14.99
VOL. 132 – COUNTRY ROCK	00701757 / $15.99
VOL. 133 – TAYLOR SWIFT	00701894 / $16.99
VOL. 134 – AVENGED SEVENFOLD	00701906 / $16.99
VOL. 136 – GUITAR THEMES	00701922 / $14.99
VOL. 137 – IRISH TUNES	00701966 / $15.99
VOL. 138 – BLUEGRASS CLASSICS	00701967 / $14.99
VOL. 139 – GARY MOORE	00702370 / $16.99
VOL. 140 – MORE STEVIE RAY VAUGHAN	00702396 / $17.99
VOL. 141 – ACOUSTIC HITS	00702401 / $16.99
VOL. 142 – KINGS OF LEON	00702418 / $16.99
VOL. 144 – DJANGO REINHARDT	00702531 / $16.99
VOL. 145 – DEF LEPPARD	00702532 / $16.99
VOL. 147 – SIMON & GARFUNKEL	14041591 / $16.99
VOL. 148 – BOB DYLAN	14041592 / $16.99
VOL. 149 – AC/DC HITS	14041593 / $17.99
VOL. 150 – ZAKK WYLDE	02501717 / $16.99
VOL. 153 – RED HOT CHILI PEPPERS	00702990 / $19.99
VOL. 156 – SLAYER	00703770 / $17.99
VOL. 157 – FLEETWOOD MAC	00101382 / $16.99
VOL. 158 – ULTIMATE CHRISTMAS	00101889 / $14.99
VOL. 160 – T-BONE WALKER	00102641/ $16.99
VOL. 161 – THE EAGLES – ACOUSTIC	00102659 / $17.99
VOL. 162 – THE EAGLES HITS	00102667 / $17.99
VOL. 163 – PANTERA	00103036 / $16.99
VOL. 166 – MODERN BLUES	00700764 / $16.99
VOL. 168 – KISS	00113421 / $16.99
VOL. 169 – TAYLOR SWIFT	00115982 / $16.99
VOL. 170 – THREE DAYS GRACE	00117337 / $16.99

Complete song lists available online.

Prices, contents, and availability subject to change without notice.

HAL•LEONARD® CORPORATION

7777 W. BLUEMOUND RD. P.O. BOX 13819 MILWAUKEE, WI 53213

www.halleonard.com

0314